EXPERT WITNESS

EXPERT WITNESS

Ellis Baker
and
Anthony Lavers

Acknowledgements

Crown copyright material is reproduced with the permission of the Controller of HMSO and the Queen's Printer for Scotland.

The text of the *Protocol for the Instruction of Experts to give Evidence in Civil Claims* is reproduced here with permission from the Civil Justice Council.

Please note: References to the masculine include, where appropriate, the feminine.

Published by RICS Business Services Limited
a wholly owned subsidiary of
The Royal Institution of Chartered Surveyors
under the RICS Books imprint
Surveyor Court
Westwood Business Park
Coventry CV4 8JE
UK

No responsibility for loss occasioned to any person acting or refraining from action as a result of the material included in this publication can be accepted by the author or publisher.

ISBN 1 84219 230 2

Typeset in Great Britain by Columns Design Ltd, Reading
Printed in Great Britain by Bell & Bain, Glasgow

Contents

Contents

Preface

Surveyors in their many different roles and specialities have more experience of acting as expert witnesses in courts, tribunals and other hearings than any other professional. For many years it has been the hallmark of a member of the Royal Institution of Chartered Surveyors (RICS) that he or she will successfully combine the role of independent witness and fearless adviser of the client with integrity and reliability.

It is therefore a particularly opportune moment for Anthony Lavers and Ellis Baker to produce this very helpful addition to the Case in Point series covering the expert witness. Surveyor experts will have received a good grounding in their role as an expert, whether it be as an expert in court, in an arbitration, adjudication or mediation, in a planning appeal, in the Lands Tribunal, as a party wall surveyor or in the many other types of tribunal that their varied practices will take them. What such an expert lacks is an authoritative and reliable guide to the practice of surveyor expert, particularly one that includes both a summary of current practice and a guide to the growing and complex case law on the subject.

It is a particular tribute to their skills as communicators that Anthony Lavers and Ellis Baker have been able to produce such a concise but reliable guide to the role of the expert witness that includes so many helpful references to the case law. It comes as no surprise that they have achieved this given their experience in this field over many years and the clarity with which they have always been able to explain this difficult area of practice.

It is particularly commendable that the book is both comprehensive and up to date. Readers will find, for example, the new (June 2005) *Protocol for the Instruction of Experts to give Evidence in Civil Claims*.

I commend this work to all surveyors and to any lawyer involved in contested dispute resolution or tribunal decision making. If you follow the guidance provided by *Case in Point: Expert Witness*, you will not go wrong and you will ensure that justice and truth will prevail.

HH Judge Thornton QC.
Technology and Construction Court.
July 2005.

Introduction

The importance of the role of the expert witness

The role of the expert witness is central to litigation, arbitration and virtually any form of dispute resolution, especially in construction, property and other areas of practice with a high technical content.

That this is not a recent idea can be seen from very early cases. In *Buckley v Rice Thomas* (1554), Mr Justice Saunders remarked that:

> '... if matters arise in our law which concern other sciences or faculties, we commonly apply for the aid of that science or faculty which it concerns, which is an honourable or commendable thing in our law. For thereby it appears that we do not despise all other sciences but our own, but we approve of them and encourage them as things worthy of our commendation'.

More than 200 years later in *Folkes v Chadd* (1782), Lord Mansfield justified the calling of an expert who:

> '... understands the construction of harbours, the causes of their destruction and how remedied. In matters of science no other witnesses can be called ... I cannot believe that where the question is, whether a defect arises from a natural or an artificial cause, the opinions of men of science are not to be received'.

Another two centuries on, in the Technology and Construction Court in *Pozzolanic Lytag Ltd v Bryan Hobson Associates* (see Section 3.1 below), the then Dyson J, deciding one of the first project management negligence cases against the background of the newly introduced *Civil Procedure Rules* 1998 (SI 1998/3132) ('CPR'), was willing to 'accept that expert witnesses fulfil a vital role in many cases'.

This last case is mentioned, however, for another reason. The judge went on to qualify his appreciation by regretting the excessive and inappropriate use of experts in a number of cases. Paradoxically, the very power which expert witnesses have come to wield over tribunals, by reason of the skill and knowledge which they can deploy, has led to controversy over the extent and nature of their involvement. The law governing these matters has therefore become a significant part of dispute resolution in itself; hence the contribution which, it is hoped, this collection of cases can offer.

Case law on the role of the expert witness

Where the expert witness is involved in litigation, the CPR apply and for this reason CPR Part 35 and its Practice Direction are included as Appendices 1 and 2 and referred to in the text which begins each section. In addition, the newly approved Civil Justice Council's *Protocol for the Instruction of Experts to give Evidence in Civil Claims* ('the Protocol') is included as Appendix 3. However, neither CPR Part 35 and its Practice Direction nor the Protocol purport to provide comprehensive rules on the role and duties of expert witnesses in given situations. It is in the cases that the legal principles were laid down and it is in the cases that their impact can actually be seen.

Case law, then, provides a major source of the law governing all aspects of the use of expert witnesses. The cases selected comprise more than 100 significant decisions of the English courts, of which half are in the areas of construction and property, reflecting the focus of the Case in Point series, as well as the authors' professional interests. The emphasis is on the role of the expert, rather than the technical rules of evidence, and on the expert's instruction, duties, expertise and potential liability, although inevitably the cases on the need for expert witnesses and their reports deal with evidential questions as well.

A balance has been sought between post-CPR decisions and those of pre-1999 date. At first sight, it might be assumed that only the former would be useful or even valid. After all, Lord Woolf himself did say, in *Ricardo Biguzzi v Rank Leisure plc* (1999), that 'Earlier authorities are no longer generally of any relevance once the CPR applies'. Coming from the then Master of the Rolls and driving force behind the CPR, that view had to be taken very seriously and hence more than 50 of the cases are post-CPR, a remarkable figure.

However, it would be too doctrinaire an approach to exclude all cases which pre-date the CPR. As Mantell LJ protested in *Daryanani v Kumar & Co* (2000), 'The old cases may no longer be relevant under the new regime but that does not mean the baby must be jettisoned with the bathwater', whilst Rimer J in *Gwembe Valley Development Co Ltd v Thomas Koshy* (2000) noted that 'Whilst I recognise that reference to pre-CPR authority on matters of practice is generally discouraged as heretical, they still afford at least a good working guide as to a just approach' (in this case to disposal of issues of costs).

It appears from May LJ in *Purdy v Cambran* (1999) and Ward LJ in *UCB Corporate Services Ltd v Halifax* (2000) that Lord Woolf's comment should be confined to cases decided *on the previous rules*, which would not govern interpretation of the CPR. It did not mean that the 'underlying thought processes' of the previous cases should be disregarded. For this reason, and because, as mentioned above, the CPR do not govern all forms of dispute resolution, a significant number of pre-1999 decisions are included, where they are of sufficient importance or offer illumination not available from anything more recent.

So the collection of cases combines classic statement of principle with the growing body of decisions on expert witnesses (and especially single joint experts) under the CPR.

Structure and use

The work is divided into the following sections and subsections:

1   Role and general duties of the expert witness
2   The duty to the tribunal of objectivity
3   Need and justification for use of expert witnesses
   3.1   The need for the expert witness
   3.2   The qualifications and experience of the expert witness
   3.3   The cost of appointing the expert witness
4   Court powers and single joint experts
   4.1   Courts' powers to allow or exclude expert evidence
   4.2   Courts' powers in relation to single joint experts
5   Pre-hearing matters
   5.1   Disclosure, confidentiality and privilege
   5.2   Meetings and agreements between expert witnesses
6   The expert witness's report
   6.1   Instructions to the expert witness

It is best used in (one or all of) three ways. Cases on individual points can be found from the index. Alternatively, each section and subsection begins with some basic text outlining its contents, which would provide a starting point on particular areas, such as 'single joint experts'. Finally, the areas from which cases are drawn are listed, so that a reader can find all cases included on, for example, 'construction, engineering and architecture' or 'valuation and surveying'.

Additionally, as has been mentioned, the CPR Part 35 Practice Direction and the Protocol also offer guidance, and are available for reference in the Appendices. Obviously, court rules do not govern disputes heard in other forums, such as arbitration.

While the purpose of providing summaries of the point of the case is convenience and accessibility, the reference is also provided in the table of cases and, where a case is seen as likely to be relevant, it is recommended that the full report be obtained, as the digested version cannot give the entire picture.

The purpose of this handbook is to raise awareness of the cases governing the work of expert witnesses and to provide initial guidance; it should not be relied upon as a substitute for proper legal advice in any given situation.

The authors are grateful to Claire Wilson and Winston Bell-Gam for assisting with collation of cases; to Mary Dodwell for suggesting a number of revisions; and to Leisa Evans for preparation of the manuscript.

List of Acts, Statutory Instruments and abbreviations

The following Acts and Statutory Instruments are referenced in this publication. Where a piece of legislation is mentioned frequently, it is referred to by the abbreviation that follows the name of the legislation in brackets.

Civil Evidence Act 1972

County Courts Act 1984

Disability Discrimination Act 1995

Environmental Protection Act 1990

Health and Safety at Work Act 1974

Housing Act 1985

Landlord and Tenant Act 1954

Limitation Act 1980

Public Health Act 1936

Supreme Court Act 1981

Town and Country Planning Act 1971

Town and Country Planning Act 1990

Civil Procedure Rules 1998 (SI 1998/3132) (**'CPR'**)

The text of this publication is divided into commentary and case summaries. The commentary is enclosed between grey highlighted lines for ease of reference.

Table of cases

List of cases by subject area

CONSTRUCTION, ENGINEERING AND ARCHITECTURE

VALUATION AND SURVEYING

PROPERTY

PERSONAL INJURY AND OTHER ACCIDENTS

NEGLIGENCE (LEGAL AND MEDICAL)

MISCELLANEOUS

1
Role and general duties of the expert witness

Beyond the overriding duty to the court in the *Civil Procedure Rules* 1998 (SI 1998/3132) ('CPR') 35.3, the CPR do not set out requirements as to the role and duties of expert witnesses, although the Practice Direction does state what is required in reports. To these may be added the assistance given in the new Civil Justice Council *Protocol for the Instruction of Experts to give Evidence in Civil Claims* ('the Protocol', see Appendix 3). The courts have endeavoured to provide detailed guidance in a number of leading judgments.

The classic statement of the duties and responsibilities of expert witnesses in civil cases was given in *National Justice Compania Naviera SA v Prudential Assurance Co Ltd: The Ikarian Reefer*. CPR Part 35, the Practice Direction and the Protocol have assimilated some of the main points of *The Ikarian Reefer*.

Specific points about the duty of objectivity in relation to obligations to the instructing client: *Polivitte Ltd v Commercial Union*; and the role of the instructing legal team: *Whitehouse v Jordan*; were adopted in *The Ikarian Reefer*.

In *Anglo Group plc v Winther Brown & Co*, the Technology and Construction Court set out the roles and duties of expert witnesses 'post-Woolf', making the point that *The Ikarian Reefer* was decided before the introduction of the CPR. This does not destroy its importance, but the *Anglo Group* case provides a significant update.

In Re J (A Minor) contains judicial observations on the duties of expert witnesses in maintaining objectivity in writing reports in particular.

As well as statements of general application, there is specific guidance on expert evidence in particular types of case; in valuation, this is provided by *English Exporters (London) Ltd v*

Eldonwall Ltd, which was discussed and applied in *Town Centre Securities Ltd v Wm Morrison Supermarkets Ltd.*

Expert witnesses are expected to understand their role and general duties, although *R v Momodou* emphasises the need to distinguish between sensible preparation and outright coaching, which might damage objectivity.

In *Re Colt Telecom Group,* the court referred to the Code of Guidance on Expert Evidence of the Working Party of the Civil Justice Council as a source on the duties of the expert witness. The Code has now been replaced by the Protocol. While it is non-statutory, it will clearly be an important source of guidance. Note also that the official RICS publication *Surveyors Acting as Expert Witnesses* includes the RICS Guidance Note and Practice Statement. Further details can be obtained on www.ricsbooks.com or from RICS Books on 0870 333 1600 (option 3).

National Justice Compania Naviera SA v Prudential Assurance Co Ltd: The Ikarian Reefer (1993)

Although this pre-CPR shipping insurance case was not regarded as deciding anything new, it is probably the most quoted single authority on the duties and responsibilities of expert witnesses, because it collected together in a form of codification the main legal principles. These are reproduced below as a list, as in the judgment, but in slightly edited form.

The duties and responsibilities of expert witnesses in civil cases include the following:

(1) Expert evidence presented to the court should be, and should be seen to be, the independent product of the expert uninfluenced as to form or content by the exigencies of litigation.

(2) An expert witness should provide independent assistance to the court by way of objective, unbiased opinion in relation to matters within his expertise. An expert witness in the High Court should never assume the role of an advocate.

(3) An expert witness should state the facts or assumptions upon which his opinion is based. He should not omit to

consider material facts which could detract from his concluded opinion.

(4) An expert witness should make it clear when a particular question or issue falls outside his expertise.

(5) If an expert's opinion is not properly researched because he considers that insufficient data is available, then this must be stated with an indication that the opinion is no more than a provisional one. In cases where an expert witness, who has prepared a report, could not assert that the report contained the truth, the whole truth and nothing but the truth without some qualification, that qualification should be stated in the report.

(6) If, after exchange of reports, an expert witness changes his view on a material matter having read the other side's expert's report or for any other reason, such change of view should be communicated (through legal representatives) to the other side without delay and when appropriate to the court.

(7) Where expert evidence refers to photographs, plans, calculations, analyses, measurements, survey reports or other similar documents, these must be provided to the opposite party at the same time as the exchange of reports.

Polivitte Ltd v Commercial Union (1987)

In a case concerning insurers' allegations of fraud in the commencement of fire at the insureds' premises, the judge offered comments on the view to be taken of the evidence of experts:

'... at the end of the day, the Court has to look at what is being asserted as a matter of (eye witness or factual) direct evidence and then to consider the integrity of that evidence ... in all the surrounding circumstances, including the impact of the expert evidence, which is (or should be) independent and, of course, based on experience and expertise ... I have almost considered the role of an expert to be two-fold: first to advance the case of the party calling him, so far as it can properly be advanced on the basis of information available to the expert in the professional exercise of his skill and experience; and, secondly, to assist the court, which does not possess the relevant skill and experience, in determining where the truth lies'.

Note that the above finding was adopted as the basis of the second point in *The Ikarian Reefer* (see this section, above).

Whitehouse v Jordan (1981)

In this medical negligence case, several of the judges expressed concern about the way in which the plaintiff's expert evidence was organised, suggesting a high degree of involvement by members of the legal team. As Lord Wilberforce put it:

'While some degree of consultation between experts and legal advisers is entirely proper, it is necessary that expert evidence presented to the court should be and should be seen to be, the independent product of the expert, uninfluenced as to form or content by the exigencies of litigation. To the extent that it is not, the evidence is likely to be not only incorrect but self defeating.'

Note that the above finding was adopted as the first point in *The Ikarian Reefer* (see this section, above).

Anglo Group plc v Winther Brown & Co (2002)

In a dispute over the sale of a computer system, the Technology and Construction Court took the opportunity to set out the role and duties of expert witnesses post-CPR, which was said to be an extension of the position set out in *The Ikarian Reefer*.

'Dispute resolution in the course of the procedure may be achieved with assistance outside the court procedure by way of independent mediation, but it may also be achieved by techniques of case management ... e.g. by "without prejudice" meetings of experts, joint statements of experts setting out the matters on which they agree or disagree, early neutral evaluation or by the appointment of a single jointly appointed expert who may effectively resolve the technical issue or issues which are preventing the parties from settling their disputes ...'

Further:

'1. An expert witness should at all stages in the procedure, on the basis of the evidence as he understands it, provide independent assistance to the court and the parties by way of objective, unbiased opinion in relation to matters within his expertise. This applies as much to the initial meetings of experts as to evidence at trial. An expert witness should never assume the role of an advocate.

2. The expert's evidence should normally be confined to technical matters on which the court will be assisted by receiving an explanation, or to evidence of common professional practice. The expert witness should not give evidence or opinions as to what the expert himself would have done in similar circumstances or otherwise seek to usurp the role of the judge.

3. He should co-operate with the expert of the other party or parties in attempting to narrow the technical issues in dispute at the earliest possible stage of the procedure and to eliminate or place in context any peripheral issues. He should co-operate with the other expert(s) in attending without prejudice meetings as necessary and in seeking to find areas of agreement and to define precisely areas of disagreement to be set out in the joint statement of experts ordered by the court.

4. The expert evidence presented to the court should be, and be seen to be, the independent product of the expert uninfluenced as to form or content by the exigencies of the litigation.

5. An expert witness should state the facts or assumptions upon which the opinion is based. He should not omit to consider material facts which could detract from his concluded opinion.

6. An expert witness should make it clear when a particular question or issue falls outside his expertise.

7. Where an expert is of the opinion that his conclusions are based on inadequate factual information, he should say so explicitly.

8.   An expert should be ready to reconsider his opinion, and if appropriate, to change his mind when he has received new information or has considered the opinion of the other expert. He should do so at the earliest opportunity.

… the new Civil Procedure Rules underline the existing duty which an expert owes to the Court as well as to the party which he represents': see *Stevens v Gullis* in Section 4.1.

'It needs to be recognised that a failure to take such an independent approach is not in the interest of the clients who retain the expert, since an expert taking a partisan approach, resulting in a failure to resolve before trial or at trial issues on which experts should agree, inflates the cost of resolving the dispute and may prevent the parties from resolving their disputes long before trial.'

In Re J (A Minor) (1990)

'Expert witnesses are in a privileged position in that they are permitted to give an opinion in evidence. Such experts have to express only genuinely held opinions which are not biased in favour of one party.

Opinions can differ but such differences are usually within a legitimate area of disagreement. An expert witness should not be misled by omission. A report should provide a straight forward not misleading opinion, be objective, should not omit factors which do not support the opinion and should have been researched properly. If the expert considers that the data available are insufficient then it has to be indicated to the court that the opinion is only provisional. An expert witness should avoid producing a report which seeks to promote a particular case as that would be an abuse of the expert's proper function and would render the report an argument not an opinion.'

Further:

'A misleading opinion will cause costs to be increased because competing evidence will have to be called. In all cases costs can be reduced if the expert witnesses on each side can discuss together their reports in advance of the hearing.'

While the above case concerned a wardship dispute, the court's observations about the general duties of expert witnesses are relevant to other types of case.

English Exporters (London) Ltd v Eldonwall Ltd (1973)

In a dispute over a *Landlord and Tenant Act* 1954 determination of interim rent under a commercial lease, the judge made a number of findings on the admissibility of evidence given by valuation expert witnesses, including evidence of transactions of which they have no first-hand knowledge:

> '... in my judgement a valuer giving expert evidence in chief (or in re-examination) –
>
> (a) may express the opinions that he has formed as to values even though substantial contributions to the formation of those opinions have been made by matters of which he has no first-hand knowledge;
>
> (b) may give evidence as to the details of any transactions within his personal knowledge, in order to establish them as matters of fact; and
>
> (c) may express his opinion as to the significance of any transactions which are or will be proved by admissible evidence (whether or not given by him) in relation to the valuation with which he is concerned; but
>
> (d) may not give hearsay evidence stating the details of any transactions not within his personal knowledge in order to establish them as matters of fact'.

Town Centre Securities Ltd v Wm Morrison Supermarkets Ltd (1982)

In a commercial rent review dispute heard in arbitration, both sides submitted evidence as to alleged valuation comparables based on hearsay evidence as to facts. It was subsequently argued that this was not admissible. The judge, noting that the objections to hearsay had not been made until after the award in an attempt to re-open the case, held that it was necessary to object to hearsay at the time when it was presented; otherwise, such evidence became admissible by agreement and it would be for the tribunal to assess the weight which should be given to it.

See *English Exporters v Eldonwall*, which was discussed and applied in the above case.

R v Momodou (2005)

Although this is a criminal law case concerning convictions for violent disorder in a detention centre, it contains a point of wider interest on the issue of witness preparation and training. Holding that 'witness training for criminal trials is prohibited', the court warned that it might affect the accuracy of evidence, especially where the training had referred to evidence or facts similar to that of a trial in which the attendee was engaged. However, this should be distinguished from 'sensible preparation', by which the witness is advised of the procedure and roles of the participants in litigation. No witness should be 'disadvantaged by ignorance of the process, nor when they come to give evidence, taken by surprise at the way it works'. The key is the 'dramatic distinction between witness training or coaching and witness familiarisation'. The former will always run the risk of influencing the evidence, while the latter, even in criminal trials, will be acceptable and even beneficial.

Re Colt Telecom Group plc (2002)

In this company insolvency case, the judge criticised an insolvency practitioner giving evidence who claimed only to have 'a general knowledge of the duty of experts'. The judge's view was that 'That is not good enough'. He advocated reference to the CPR Part 35 Practice Direction and to the Code of Guidance.

Note: The Practice Direction is reproduced at Appendix 2 of this handbook. The Code of Guidance was replaced, as from 5 September 2005, by the *Protocol for the Instruction of Experts to give Evidence in Civil Claims* (see Appendix 3).

2
The duty to the tribunal of objectivity

CPR 35.3 makes clear that the duty of an expert witness is to the court and will override any obligations to the person paying the expert. This is expanded in paras 1.1 to 1.4 of the Practice Direction. Other tribunals (for example, in arbitration) will normally expect such objectivity and assistance, even if the requirement is not made equally explicit.

For many years, judges have complained about the tendency of some expert witnesses to forsake objectivity and to argue the case of their clients in the manner of an advocate. This phenomenon is not confined to any one discipline.

The section contains examples:

From valuation:

- *Arab Bank plc v John D Wood (Commercial) Ltd;*
- *Cemp Properties (UK) Ltd v Dentsply Research and Development Corporation;*
- *Clonard Developments Ltd v Humberts;*
- *Reynolds v Manchester City Council;* and
- *Shortlands Investments Ltd v Cargill plc.*

From planning:

- *Burroughs Day v Bristol City Council;* and
- *Multi Media Productions Ltd v Secretary of State.*

From architecture and construction:

- *Cala Homes (South) v Alfred McAlpine Homes East Ltd;*
- *Pearce v Ove Arup Partnership;* and
- *Great Eastern Hotel Co Ltd v John Laing Co Ltd.*

In architecture see also *Royal Brompton NHS Trust v Hammond* in Section 3.2 and *University of Warwick v Sir Robert McAlpine* in Section 6.2.

The reasons for the departure from objectivity vary. In *Cala Homes (South) v Alfred McAlpine Homes East Ltd*, the architect expert witness had, in a published article, explored the possibility that the judge was 'fair game' to an expert. No doubt often the expert will feel under pressure from the client, and in *Reynolds v Manchester City Council* the Chairman of the Lands Tribunal noted that the expert's valuation figures had been adopted after discussion with his client, the expert not having seen the (demolished) property. In the planning cases of *Burroughs Day v Bristol City Council* and *Multi Media Productions Ltd v Secretary of State*, the expert witnesses were planning officers appearing on behalf of the authorities which employed them, in the latter case actually combining the role of advocate with that of expert witness. The possibility of such a dual role has been recognised by the RICS Practice Statement *Surveyors Acting as Expert Witnesses*, but the difficulty of meeting the objectivity requirement is obvious. That even an objective manner is important appears from *Shortlands Investments Ltd v Cargill plc*. A refusal to revise an opinion in the light of new information gives an appearance of intransigence and attracted criticism from the court in *Great Eastern Hotel v John Laing*.

Personal relationships between experts and parties to an action are another potential cause of loss of objectivity and this issue is considered in *Liverpool Roman Catholic Archdiocesan Trust v Goldberg* and *R v Secretary of State for Transport ex parte Factortame*. It should not, however, be assumed that *any* personal involvement automatically debars the giving of expert evidence: in *David Michael Lusty v Finsbury Securities Ltd*, an architect's evidence as to the reasonableness of his own fees was held to be admissible.

The consequence of departure from objectivity is usually that the evidence is deprived of most or all of its weight: *Cala Homes (South) v Alfred McAlpine Homes East Ltd*, *Cemp Properties v Dentsply* and *Reynolds v Manchester City Council*. On the extreme facts of *Pearce v Ove Arup Partnership Ltd*, the expert was actually reported to his professional body, although it is understood that he was later exonerated.

Arab Bank plc v John D Wood (Commercial) Ltd (1998)

In this negligent valuation case (which also went to the Court
of Appeal, whose decision does not affect the point below),
the judge complained of the lack of objectivity exhibited by
the valuation expert witnesses:

'The court has not been assisted by the tendency which I
detected in all the expert witnesses who gave evidence
before me to take upon their own shoulders the mantle of
advocacy and themselves to seek to persuade the court to
a desired result rather than to offer dispassionate and
disinterested assistance and advice to the court to enable it
to arrive at a fair and balanced view of the conflicting
contentions of the parties.'

Burroughs Day v Bristol City Council (1996)

Hearing an application for a declaration that proposed
building works did not constitute 'development' for the
purposes of the *Town and Country Planning Act* 1990, the
judge criticised the lack of independence of the expert
witnesses called by the local planning authority.

'... it is not the role of an expert in a case such as this to
express opinions as to the interpretation of statutory
provisions. The expert evidence adduced before me went
this far: indeed one town planning witness called by the
council went further and decided that an estoppel pleaded
by the solicitors ... did not arise. This represented a
misuse of expert evidence and showed a
misunderstanding of the role of an expert witness in a
case such as this ...

The Council adduced the evidence of two witnesses
described as "expert witnesses" ... Both were long-serving
employees of the council (though (one) was now retired)
and were not in any sense independent experts. Both
appeared to regard advocacy for their employer as an
integral part of their role as an expert. Both expressed
opinions on statutory interpretation ... I can give only
limited weight to any of their evidence'.

Approving the guidance in *The Ikarian Reefer*, the judge indicated three conclusions on the present case:

'(1) Some of the expert witnesses were not independent, being employees or ex-employees of the council.

(2) Some of the expert witnesses apparently thought that it was an essential part of their function as experts to act as supplementary advocates for their clients, the council.

(3) Each of the expert witnesses, who were architects or town planners, took it upon himself to reach conclusions as to the interpretation of the statutory provisions, a matter on which expert opinion from a non-lawyer is neither admissible nor helpful.'

Cala Homes (South) v Alfred McAlpine Homes East Ltd (1995)

In the course of litigation over copyright of standard house designs, it was revealed that the defendants' expert witness, an eminent architect, had written an article in the *Journal of the Chartered Institute of Arbitrators* entitled 'The Expert Witness: Partisan with a Conscience', in which he compared the role of the expert witness with that of the 'man who works the Three Card Trick' who 'is not cheating, nor does he incur any moral opprobrium, when he uses his sleight of hand to deceive the eye of the innocent rustic and to deny him the information he needs for a correct appraisal of what has gone on'.

The judge condemned this approach in forthright terms:

'The function of a court of law is to discover the truth relating to the issues before it. In doing that it has to assess the evidence adduced by the parties. The judge is not a rustic who has chosen to play a game of Three Card Trick. He is not fair game. Nor is the truth. ... An expert should not consider that it is his job to stand shoulder-to-shoulder through thick and thin with the side that is paying his bill.'

In the light of these findings, the judge had re-read the expert's report,

'... on the understanding that it was drafted as a partisan tract with the objective of selling the defendant's case to the court and ignoring virtually everything which could harm that objective. I did not find it of significant assistance in deciding the issues'.

Cemp Properties (UK) Ltd v Dentsply Research and Development Corporation (1991)

In an action for misrepresentation allegedly inducing the purchaser to enter into a contract to buy a property, the court criticised the valuation expert witnesses, whose evidence had been understandably rejected by the first instance judge.

'... it is a sad feature of modern litigation that expert witnesses, particularly in valuation cases, instead of giving evidence of their actual views as to the true position, enter into the arena and, as advocates, put forward the maximum or minimum figures as best suited to their sides interests. If experts do this, they must not be surprised if their views carry little weight with the judge. In this case, such evidence rightly led the judge to reject the expert evidence on both sides'.

Clonard Developments Ltd v Humberts (1999)

In a negligent valuation case, the appellant developers challenged the first instance judge's description of their valuation expert witness as 'unhampered by impartiality'. The Court of Appeal upheld the judge's right to reach such a finding and rejected the appellant's criticism:

'A judge sitting at first instance must always be astute to the possibility that the expert before him may not be fulfilling his role as an impartial or objective adviser and is seeking to espouse the cause for which he has been instructed.'

The first instance judge in this case

'... was clearly left with the firm impression that, consciously or unconsciously, the experts had ceased to be impartial, were espousing the cause and thus assuming the role of advocate. If this were his perception it was his duty to say so and to act accordingly by rejecting or discounting those parts of their evidence which was so tainted'.

David Michael Lusty v Finsbury Securities Ltd (1991)

In a claim by an architect for professional fees, the defendant client argued that the architect's evidence as to the value of his work was inadmissible, because he was an interested party. The Court of Appeal rejected this argument. The fact that Mr Lusty was an interested party could only, at most, affect the weight given to his evidence and not its admissibility:

> 'If every time a professional man sued for his fees he had to have some independent evidence for what he himself considered to be his proper fees it would clearly be intolerable. He must be fully entitled to give his own view to the court and to see whether the court accepts that view ...'

Great Eastern Hotel Co Ltd v John Laing Co Ltd (2005)

In this case an alleged breach of obligation by the defendant construction manager was the subject of an action by the clients. The judge criticised the evidence of the defendants' expert witness as 'lacking in thoroughness in his research and unreliable by reason of his uncritical acceptance of the favourable accounts put forward by Laing'. The judge especially remarked upon the expert's failure to revise his opinion in the light of facts subsequently becoming apparent.

Liverpool Roman Catholic Archdiocesan Trust v Goldberg (2001)

An issue arose in an action (later compromised) as to the admissibility of the evidence of an expert who was a colleague of the defendant in the same chambers, and a close friend. The judge held that

> '... where it is demonstrated that there exists a relationship between the proposed expert and the party calling him which a reasonable observer might think was capable of affecting the views of the expert so as to make them unduly favourable to that party, his evidence should not be admitted however unbiased the conclusions of the expert might probably be'.

However, see below in this section, *R v Secretary of State for Transport ex parte Factortame*, doubting the accuracy of the above summary.

Multi Media Productions Ltd v Secretary of State for Environment and Islington LBC (1989)

In an application to the High Court under the *Town and Country Planning Act* 1971 by a developer against dismissal of its appeal against refusal of planning permission, the judge made a number of findings on procedural fairness. The Case Editor for the *Journal of Planning and Environment Law*, Professor Michael Purdue, noted that the judge 'placed less weight on the planning officer's evidence because he had combined the role of witness with that of advocate at the inquiry'. This refers to a local planning inquiry where a planner or, for example, a chartered surveyor, might be allowed to combine the roles.

The possibility of such a dual role is expressly recognised by the RICS Practice Statement *Surveyors Acting as Expert Witnesses*, for example in valuation tribunals, rent assessment committees or hearings before independent experts. However, courts have frequently criticised any tendency of experts to adopt the mantle of advocacy: see *University of Warwick v Sir Robert McAlpine* and *Cala Homes v Alfred McAlpine*. On the use by councils of their officers as expert witnesses, see *Field v Leeds City Council* in Section 3.2.

Pearce v Ove Arup Partnership Ltd (2001)

The claimant architect alleged that the design by Rem Koolhaas of the famous Kunsthal art gallery in Rotterdam had been plagiarised from his final year project at the Architectural Association for a town hall in London Docklands. The judge, in dismissing the claim, made a number of criticisms of the evidence and lack of objectivity of the architect expert witness called by the claimant. One such criticism was that the expert had not visited the Kunsthal before making his report, and had not mentioned this fact in the report. Another was that the expert had not read properly a document which he annexed to his report. The judge concluded that the expert witness did not understand his duty to help the court, overriding his obligation to his client:

> 'He came to argue a case. Any point which might support that case, however flimsy, he took. Nowhere did he stand back and take an objective view as an architect as to how the alleged copying could have been done. [The expert witness] bears a heavy responsibility for this case ever coming to trial – with its attendant cost, expense and waste of time ...'

The judge noted that 'there is no rule for specific sanctions where an expert witness is in breach of his Part 35 duty ... there is no specific accrediting body to whose attention a breach of the duty can be drawn'. However, the judge noted that many expert witnesses, including this one, belong to a professional body:

> 'I see no reason why a judge who has formed the opinion that an expert has seriously broken his Part 35 duty should not, in an appropriate case, refer the matter to the expert's professional body if he or she has one. Whether there is a breach of the expert's professional rules and if so what sanction is appropriate would be a matter for the body concerned.'

In the result, failing adequate representations within 21 days from the expert as to why he should not do so, the judge asked the defendants' solicitors to refer the matter to the Royal Institute of British Architects (RIBA).

Note: It is understood that the RIBA exonerated the expert witness from any professional misconduct.

R v Secretary of State for Transport ex parte Factortame (2002)

> 'It is always desirable that an expert should have no actual or apparent interest in the outcome of the proceedings in which he gives evidence, but such disinterest is not automatically a precondition to the admissibility of his evidence. Where an expert has an interest of one kind or

another in the outcome of the case, this fact should be made known to the court as soon as possible. The question of whether the proposed expert should be permitted to give evidence should then be determined in the course of case management. In considering that question the Judge will have to weigh the alternative choices open if the expert's evidence is excluded, having regard to the overriding objective of the Civil Procedure Rules.'

Note that the above case should be regarded as generally more authoritative than *Liverpool Roman Catholic Archdiocese Trust v Goldberg* which was criticised by the Court of Appeal on this point.

Reynolds v Manchester City Council (1981)

In a dispute over valuation of compensation for compulsory purchase, the Chairman of the Tribunal explained why he felt obliged to discount the evidence of the claimant's expert.

The claimant's expert

'… relied neither on comparables nor on his own experience in his evidence-in-chief and also in cross-examination [the expert] was explicit not only that he had never seen the subject property prior to its demolition but also that the figures appearing in his valuation had been adopted after discussion with [the claimant] … This being the foundation of his valuation, I regret that I can attach no weight to [the expert's] evidence. Valuation is a matter of independent uninfluenced judgment. Opinion evidence given at second-hand is not really evidence at all'.

See also *R v Balfour Beatty* in Section 6.2.

Shortlands Investments Ltd v Cargill plc (1995)

In a claim for dilapidations on the termination of a tenancy of office premises, the judge contrasted the demeanour and effectiveness of the respective expert witnesses giving valuation evidence. The defendants' valuer was:

'... an expert who came on the scene fairly recently. His evidence was strongly argumentative without always having the support of logic. He was very ready to draw inferences adverse to the [claimants] from documents which he read only after the event'.

By contrast, the claimants' valuer:

'... seemed to be a very honest witness as to the facts of which he had first hand knowledge ... he gave his evidence of opinion modestly and with a willingness to make proper concessions and his evidence appeared logical and sensible'.

The evidence of the claimants' valuer was preferred when there was a conflict of opinion.

3
Need and justification for use of expert witnesses

Under CPR 35.4(1), no party may call expert evidence without the court's permission. It therefore follows that there must always be a demonstrable need for the expert witness and a justification of the expense involved in the expert's participation in the proceedings. This will be true of any tribunal, whether or not the limitation is made express, since costs wasted can hardly be recovered, setting aside the expenditure of time and effort.

This section is divided into three parts:

3.1 The need for the expert witness
3.2 The qualifications and experience of the expert witness
3.3 The cost of appointing the expert witness

3.1 THE NEED FOR THE EXPERT WITNESS

Under CPR 35.1, 'Expert evidence shall be restricted to that which is reasonably required to resolve the proceedings'.

There is therefore a preliminary question to be asked as to whether particular, or indeed any, expert evidence is required in a particular case. A court may refuse an application for permission to call a specific expert, for example, because of delay; procedural orders of this kind are dealt with in Section 4.1 below. However, in this subsection the issues are more fundamental, such as whether an area of knowledge can properly be regarded as expertise at all, or whether evidence makes any contribution to the resolution of the dispute.

In *Baldev Singh Mann v Chetty & Patel*, the Court of Appeal offers guidance as to the factors determining entitlement to call expert evidence, namely: cogency, helpfulness and cost.

There are certain types of case in which expert evidence is normally regarded as necessary, such as professional negligence actions: *Worboys v Acme Investments Ltd.*

However, even here the matter is not completely straightforward. If the expert is being asked to decide on the extent of a professional's duty, that may be a matter of law and therefore 'the very question which it is the court's function to decide': *Midland Bank Trust Co Ltd v Hett Stubbs & Kemp* and *Barings plc v Coopers & Lybrand*. This 'ultimate issue' is considered further in Section 7.1 below. Paradoxically, but probably inevitably, this preliminary consideration is sometimes not properly resolved until judgment is given. In *Pozzolanic Lytag Ltd v Bryan Hobson Associates* consulting engineers had thus been allowed to give evidence on contributory negligence – a matter of law.

More usually, the complaint of the court is not that *no* expert evidence was necessary, but that the experts selected were inappropriate. In *Rawlinson v Westbrook* the 'totally absurd' costs could have been avoided if the (chartered surveyor) parties had given evidence themselves, instead of instructing experts.

Where the lack of justification is obvious at the outset, the court can prevent the waste by refusing leave to call the expert, but where the partial or total uselessness of the evidence only becomes apparent as it is given, penalisation in costs is the likely consequence, as in *Mitchell v Mulholland* and *Phillips v Symes.*

On the specific question of 'witness shopping', the court in *Thorn v Worthing Skating Rink Co* doubted the value of an expert obtained by such a method.

Baldev Singh Mann v Chetty & Patel (2000)

Following a matrimonial dispute, the appellant had sued his solicitors for professional negligence. The judge refused him permission to adduce expert evidence as to valuation of the matrimonial home, as to valuation of a business in which he had been a partner and as to allegedly forged handwriting. The Court of Appeal considered the entitlement to call expert evidence:

'Expert evidence is to be restricted to that which is reasonably required to resolve the proceedings (rule 35.1). No party may call expert evidence without the court's permission (rule 35.4(1)). The court may direct that evidence be given by a single joint expert instructed by the parties (rule 35.7) or appoint an assessor to assist the court (rule 35.15).

Clearly, therefore the court has to make a judgment on at least three matters: (a) how cogent the proposed expert evidence will be; (b) how helpful it will be in resolving any of the issues in the case; and (c) how much it will cost and the relationship of that cost to the sums at stake.'

In the circumstances, the court upheld the decision to refuse leave to call expert evidence as to valuation of the matrimonial home and as to handwriting, but allowed the appeal against refusal to permit evidence to be given as to the value and profitability of the business.

Worboys v Acme Investments Ltd (1969)

In a dispute between an architect and his clients, the latter made allegations of professional negligence against the former. The clients called as expert a surveyor who gave evidence as to what the cost of remedial work ought to have been. The court held that there was no evidence to support a finding of professional negligence. Counsel for the clients argued that 'this is a class of case in which the court can find a breach of professional duty without having before it the standard type of evidence as to what constitutes lack of care on the part of a professional man in the relevant circumstances'. The court rejected this argument:

'There may well be cases in which it would be not necessary to adduce such evidence – as, for instance, if an architect omitted to provide a front door to the premises. But it would be grossly unfair to architects if, on a point of the type now under consideration, which relates to a special type of dwelling, the courts could without the normal evidence condemn a professional man.'

The then editors of the *Building Law Reports*, now His Honour Humphrey LLoyd QC and Colin Reese QC, commented on this case that:

'... the evidence should normally come from someone who is of equal experience or standing to the professional man in question, although evidence from a person who is acquainted with the standards may also suffice. For example, if the issue relates to a matter of structural design, evidence from a structural engineer may well be acceptable as to the standards of an architect who has undertaken the structural design'.

But see on this last point *Sansom v Metcalfe Hambleton* in Section 3.2.

Midland Bank Trust Co Ltd v Hett Stubbs & Kemp (1978)

In a professional negligence action brought against a firm of solicitors for failing to protect a client's property interest by timely registration, the judge called into question the value of the evidence offered by solicitor expert witnesses in such a case:

'I must say that I doubt the value, or even the admissibility, of this sort of evidence, which seems to be becoming customary in cases of this type. The extent of the legal duty in any given situation must, I think, be a question of law for the court. Clearly if there is some practice in a particular profession, some accepted standard of conduct which is laid down by a professional institute or sanctioned by common usage, evidence of that can and ought to be received. But evidence which really amounts to no more than an expression of opinion by a particular practitioner of what he thinks that he would have done had he been placed, hypothetically and without the benefit of hindsight, in the position of the defendants, is of little assistance to the court; whilst evidence of the witnesses' view of what, as a matter of law, the solicitor's duty was in the particular circumstances of the case is, I should have thought, inadmissible, for that is the very question which it is the court's function to decide.'

Note: The 'very question which it is the court's function to decide' is sometimes described as the 'ultimate issue'. See

Crosfield (Joseph) and Sons v Techno-Chemical Laboratories in Section 7.1 which also adopts a hard line on the 'ultimate issue'; but see more recently *Barings plc v Coopers & Lybrand,* which illustrates a modern modification of this position.

Barings plc (in liquidation) v Coopers & Lybrand (2001)

In part of the litigation relating to the liquidation of Barings, following the Leeson scandal (in which the bank sustained heavy losses through fraudulent practices by one of its employees), objection was taken by Barings to the calling of expert evidence regarding banking management. Barings argued that criticism of their management, based on opinion, was not expert evidence. The court held that the overall purpose of expert evidence is to enable the court to reach a fully informed decision.

> 'It is for the party seeking to call expert evidence to satisfy the court that expert evidence is available which would have a bearing on the issues which the Court has to decide and would be helpful to the Court in coming to a conclusion on those issues.'

Further:

> '... expert evidence is admissible under section 3 of the Civil Evidence Act 1972 in any case where the Court accepts that there exists a recognised expertise governed by recognised standards and rules of conduct capable of influencing the Court's decision on any of the issues which it has to decide and the witness to be called satisfies the Court that he has a sufficient familiarity with and knowledge of the expertise in question to render his opinion potentially of value in resolving any of those issues'.

However,

> 'Evidence meeting this test can still be excluded by the Court if the Court takes the view that calling it will not be helpful to the Court in resolving any issue in the case justly.'

In this case, the court was satisfied that there was a 'body of expertise with recognised standards in relation to the management of investment banks'. It would be 'very significant that this is an area of commerce which is highly regulated, practitioners in which are required to be licensed by the regulator and in respect of which the regulator has prescribed standards of prescribed competence'. The court did not regard it as fatal to the validity of the evidence that the experts also appeared to answer the 'ultimate issue' as to whether the defendants were negligent. Nor were criticisms of the 'forceful language' used by the experts sufficient to prevent them being called:

> 'If it emerges from the cross-examination of the Defendants experts on banking practice that the views they have expressed are overly tendentious and partisan that would go to undermine the authority of those views in the eyes of the Court. These objections are not a reason for striking out any part of the Defendant's expert reports at this stage.'

Pozzolanic Lytag Ltd v Bryan Hobson Associates (1998)

In this case, concerning allegations of professional negligence by a project manager in failing to check that contractors' insurance was in place, the court criticised the extent of the expert evidence tendered, especially the length of the experts' reports. The judge hoped that the then-imminent implementation of the Woolf reforms in the CPR would focus attention on the cost of excessive use of experts.

> 'Of course I accept that expert witnesses fulfil a vital role in many cases. I strongly suspect, however, that in many cases insufficient thought is given by parties (and in particular their legal representatives) first to the question whether an expert is really necessary at all, and secondly to what issues the evidence of the expert should be directed.
>
> … The Official Referee was persuaded to give leave for experts, but his order confined them to giving evidence about the common practice in the construction industry as to the role of consulting engineers, in particular in relation to the insurance of risks between employer and contractor. He also (and surprisingly) allowed the experts to deal with the question whether there had been contributory negligence by [the claimants]. It seems to me that the issue of contributory negligence by [the

claimants] is one with which the engineer experts should plainly not have been concerned.

... the only issue to which expert evidence could properly have been directed was whether there is a common practice in the engineering profession as to what engineers, who are engaged as project managers, do in relation to the insurance obligations of contractors. That would have been a short point, which should have resulted in short reports. Instead of this, the experts prepared quite elaborate reports dealing with a number of other issues, which were inappropriate ... [The claimant's expert] reviewed some of the correspondence in the case. [The defendant's expert] produced a report which runs to 44 pages (excluding annexures), much of which is taken up with a recitation of the events and extracts from the correspondence.

The experts plainly went well beyond what the Official Referee had authorised ... Prolix experts' reports directed to issues with which they should not be concerned merely add to the expense of litigation. Everything possible should be done to discourage this. In appropriate cases, this will include making special orders for costs.'

Rawlinson v Westbrook (1995)

The Court of Appeal deplored the fact that the Rules of the Supreme Court, in this pre-CPR case, did not allow judges and masters to refuse to allow any expert evidence to be given at trial of an action. The judge was able to limit the number of experts, but not exclude such evidence altogether.

Judges and masters were 'frequently forced to observe the spectacle of litigants like lemmings rushing to their own doom by engaging too many and unnecessary experts ... every litigant thought, or at least his solicitor did, that he had to have at least one expert called to give evidence for him'.

In this case, involving a dispute over fees for professional services, 'There had been no need for any expert evidence to be called at all: both the parties were chartered surveyors who could have given the relevant evidence themselves'. The result was that the taxed costs of the hearing before the judge were 'totally absurd'.

Mitchell v Mulholland (1973)

The claimant sued for damages caused in a car crash for which the defendants were admittedly responsible. He called an actuary and a chartered accountant as expert witnesses on loss of earnings and an economist to provide evidence on the prospects of future inflation. Neither the trial judge nor the Court of Appeal was satisfied that these experts offered a more reliable method of calculation than the traditional multiplier method used by the courts. The Court of Appeal was asked to consider the costs award for these witnesses, given that the claimant had won, but that their evidence had been largely inadmissible.

'The evidence of the economist had been neither necessary nor proper, so specious had been his testimony, and all the costs of his evidence should be disallowed. There had been some residual, though limited, value in calling the actuary and the chartered accountant, and it had not been wholly unreasonable to call them. But as they had based their evidence largely on that of the economist it had reached far more expansive dimensions than it would otherwise have done. The [claimant] should recover only one third of the cost of calling them.'

Phillips v Symes (2004)

In an action to recover costs, where the mental capacity of the defendant was in issue, the claimants sought to join the defendant's expert witness, a consultant psychiatrist. The court held that it had power to make a costs order against an expert witness who caused significant expense to be incurred by giving his evidence in flagrant disregard of his duties to the court. No special warning to the expert was necessary.

'The only warning required to be given to an expert is the self evident one set out in the Civil Procedure Rules and the declaration or statement of truth set out in paragraph 2.4 of Practice Direction 35, which the expert had to verify.

That declaration warns the expert, in effect that he can be subjected to contempt proceedings if he gives false evidence. Therefore, in the context of an expert witness, no further warning is required.

Although there are sanctions available against such experts who breach their duties to the court, those are ineffective in some circumstances, where the proper sanction is the ability to compensate the person who has suffered loss by reason of the evidence given.'

3.2 THE QUALIFICATIONS AND EXPERIENCE OF THE EXPERT WITNESS

Generally, the courts take the view that an expert witness may be qualified by skill or experience as well as by academic or professional qualifications: *Longley v South West Regional Health Authority* and *Ajami v Comptroller of Customs*. Equally, while in valuation market knowledge will always be advantageous, information can be obtained through proper preparation: *Abbey National Mortgages v Key Surveyors Nationwide Ltd.*

Once the court is satisfied that an area of expertise actually exists, someone with practical experience in it can be called as an expert. In *Barings v Coopers & Lybrand* (see Section 3.1), the area in dispute was that of banking management. An environmental health officer was not required to possess medical qualifications to give evidence as to whether the state of premises was prejudicial to health: *O'Toole v Knowsley Metropolitan Borough Council*.

Recent, rather than out-of-date, experience will usually be expected: *Royal Brompton NHS Trust v Hammond*.

However, none of the above means that qualifications are irrelevant. It would be impossible to decide if a council officer could give evidence without knowing his qualifications and experience: *Field v Leeds City Council*; this would also apply to any potential expert. The CPR Part 35 Practice Direction, at para. 2.2.1, requires the expert's report to contain details of qualifications.

Furthermore, in the particular category of professional negligence cases, the discipline of the expert witness will be crucial. Expert evidence is almost always essential in a professional negligence case: *Worboys v Acme Investments* in Section 3.1; but that evidence must be provided by someone from the same profession as the defendant. Thus engineers cannot provide valid evidence, for example, of the competence of architects or surveyors: *Investors in Industry v South Bedfordshire District Council, Sansom v Metcalfe Hambleton & Co* and *Whalley v Roberts & Roberts.*

Longley v South West Regional Health Authority (1983)

In a dispute over the fees claimed by an expert witness appearing as a claims consultant in an arbitration, the judge had to consider the status of the expert. The respondent Health Authority argued that, since the claims consultant had no professional qualification, for example, in quantity surveying, he could not be considered an expert. The judge held the argument to be 'groundless': 'An expert may be qualified by skill or experience, as well as by professional qualification.'

It was also argued that he was not an expert witness since he had not actually been called before the arbitration settled in mid-hearing. The fact that the claimants' solicitor could show that the witness would have been called at the end of the trial on the schedules he had prepared disposed of that argument.

The final argument was that such an expert was superfluous before an arbitrator who was himself an expert in the subject. The judge rejected this: 'One reason for having an expert arbitrator is so that he should be able to understand the expert evidence, not so that he should have to do without it.'

Ajami v Comptroller of Customs (1954)

The Privy Council held that a branch bank manager, engaged in banking business in Nigeria for 24 years, had to, and did, maintain a current knowledge of banknotes in use in West Africa. He was therefore to be regarded as an expert giving expert evidence. The appellants had maintained that this was a matter on which no non-lawyer could be regarded as a competent expert, but the court rejected this:

'... not only the general nature, but also the precise character of the question upon which expert evidence is required, have to be taken into account when deciding whether the qualifications of a person entitle him to be regarded as a competent expert. So the practical knowledge of a person who is not a lawyer may be sufficient in certain cases to qualify him as a competent expert on a question of foreign law'.

Abbey National Mortgages plc v Key Surveyors Nationwide Ltd (1995)

The claimant lender sued the defendant valuers in respect of valuations of 29 properties in different parts of the country. The defendants argued that a separate expert would be needed for each party for each of the 29 properties, because of the need for personal knowledge and experience of local market conditions. The claimants argued for a single court expert to be appointed. The court held that there should be no presumption either for or against the appointment of a court expert. (Note that this decision was pre-CPR.) The crucial factor in deciding would be whether it would assist in the just, expeditious and economical disposal of the action: the court 'is concerned with doing justice, not with achieving a state of expensive and unnecessary perfection'. In the result, it would not be necessary to have a separate expert for each property; the necessary market knowledge could be obtained through proper preparation.

O'Toole v Knowsley Metropolitan Borough Council (1999)

This was an appeal by way of case stated from a decision of the Knowsley justices that premises were not in a state 'prejudicial to health or a nuisance' under section 79(1)(a) of the *Environmental Protection Act* 1990. The justices had excluded evidence as to prejudice to health given by former environmental health officers acting as consultants on the ground that, while competent on matters of condition of the premises, they could not give expert evidence on the occupiers' state of health.

The court accepted the appellants' submission that 'it was not necessary for the environmental health officers to possess medical qualifications in order to express an opinion as to whether or not the premises were prejudicial to health as defined by section 79(1)(a) of the Act'.

The finding was that: 'The Environmental Health Officers possessed appropriate knowledge and expertise which the Justices did not have. By refusing to accept the evidence of those witnesses, the Justices substituted their own view on this issue which they were not entitled to do.' The appeal was accordingly allowed.

See *Patel v Mehtab* which was approved in the above case.

Royal Brompton NHS Trust v Hammond (No 7) (2001)

The judge held that an architect expert witness, in this case of alleged negligent construction contract administration, had produced a report in which the conclusions led inevitably from the assumptions he had been instructed to make by his clients. This fatally undermined the objectivity of the evidence.

The judge also noted that the expert witness had not practised as an architect in the previous 12 years, having sold his interest in his firm in 1988; since then he had 'not practised as an architect in the ordinary sense, but rather as a consultant and professional expert witness'. The effect of this was that 'it could be said of his evidence that it was not that of someone who had experience of the practices of architects at the time relevant to the issues raised'. Whereas in some civil law jurisdictions, experts are expected to be very senior and therefore often retired from practice, lack of current experience of an expert witness will be a potential weakness in an English trial, or other hearing, where the subject matter is professional standards prevailing at the time of the alleged negligence.

Field v Leeds City Council (2000)

In proceedings by tenants against the council, their landlords, for breach of repair obligations and statutory nuisance, the district judge refused to allow the council to use as an expert witness a person employed in their housing services claims investigation department. The council appealed against that refusal. Lord Woolf MR in the Court of Appeal accepted that 'if an expert is properly qualified to give evidence, then the fact that he is employed by a local authority would not disqualify him from giving evidence'. However, in such a case, without knowing more about the officer's experience, qualifications and the actual nature of his employment, the judge would have been unable to decide whether he was an appropriate expert witness. He had not yet written any report and the council offered no evidence as to these matters. More generally, if a council wishes to use an officer in this role,

'... it is important that they show that he has full knowledge of the requirements for an expert to give evidence before the court, and that he is fully familiar with the need for objectivity ... I would encourage ... the authority concerned to provide some training for such a person to which they can point to show that he has the necessary awareness of the difficult role of an expert ...'.

Investors In Industry Ltd v South Bedfordshire District Council (1986)

In an action in which the negligence of a firm of architects was alleged, the expert evidence before the judge was given by three engineers and one architect. The Court of Appeal noted that the questions put to the engineers and answered by them included questions relating to the nature and extent of the professional duties owed by the architects to their clients. The court's conclusion was that 'little reliance can be placed on their answers to these particular questions, which relate to a profession other than their own'.

Sansom v Metcalfe Hambleton & Co (1998)

Where the defendant chartered surveyor had been found negligent in failure to draw attention to a crack in a building, the Court of Appeal held that this finding could not be supported by reference to the evidence of a structural engineer:

'... a court should be slow to find a professionally qualified man guilty of a breach of his duty of skill and care towards a client (or third party) without evidence from those within the same profession as to the standard expected on the facts of the case and the failure of the professionally qualified man to measure up to that standard. It is not an absolute rule ... but, unless it is an obvious case, in the absence of the relevant expert evidence the claim will not be proved'.

Whalley v Roberts & Roberts (1990)

In a professional negligence claim brought against chartered surveyors in respect of a residential valuation, both parties called as expert witnesses representatives of other professions: a civil engineer for the claimants and an architect for the defendants, as well as a chartered surveyor on each side. The judge held that on the issue of negligence by the defendants 'it is only the evidence of the surveyors ... that may be of value on this issue'. The civil engineer and the architect 'however competent they may be in their respective professions, cannot speak with authority on what is to be expected of the ordinarily competent surveyor'.

The court applied *Investors in Industry v South Bedfordshire* on this point.

3.3 THE COST OF APPOINTING THE EXPERT WITNESS

As with other aspects of the need for appointing an expert witness, the cost must be justifiable. The key here is that it must be proportionate, both to the sum in dispute and to the contribution which the expert's evidence will make. Thus the court in *Abbey National Mortgages v Key Surveyors* (see Section 3.2) would not permit the appointment of a separate valuation expert for each of 29 properties in dispute in any effort to reach 'a state of expensive and unnecessary perfection'. And in a dispute over the value of a car, a published guide from a newsagent would be preferable to 'the expensive calling of two live experts': *Bandegani v Norwich Union Fire Insurance Society*.

The emphasis in the courts is on the parties and their experts themselves exercising discipline and restraint and 'a sense of proportion': *The Pelopidas and TRSL Concord*; see also *Graigola Merthyr Co Ltd v Swansea Corporation* in Section 5.2 on narrowing issues to minimise costs.

Under CPR 35.4(4), the court has the power to place a limit on the amount of an expert's recoverable fees and expenses: *Kranidiotes v Paschali*.

Failure to observe the need for attention to economy is typically penalised in costs: *Mitchell v Mulholland* in Section 3.1. A costs order can be made against an expert in appropriate cases: *Phillips v Symes* in Section 3.1.

Bandegani v Norwich Union Fire Insurance Society Ltd (1999)

The appellant had sued his insurer, the Norwich Union, which had offered only £900 under a motor policy following the destruction of the appellant's car, for which he had paid £1,500 four months earlier. Neither side had sent any expert report to the other, but the Norwich Union sent a witness to the court on the morning of the trial. The appellant had requested an adjournment, but the judge refused this, saying that he would not take the evidence of the witness, a claims engineer employed by Norwich Union, into account. The judge ruled that there was no evidence as to value, and the claim failed.

The Court of Appeal rejected the appellant's first submission, that the judge had actually taken the evidence into account and also that the request for an adjournment had been wrongly refused. However, the judge had been wrong in law to discount the evidence provided by the sale four months earlier as to market value, especially as expert evidence should be discouraged in such cases. Accordingly, the appeal was allowed.

'I quite accept that the price someone has recently paid for a secondhand item may not be very strong evidence of its value and that it may be displaced by other reliable evidence that the true market value is different. (In a case of this kind, namely a small claims arbitration in relation to a car, by referring to "other reliable evidence" I am not envisaging expert evidence but simply the sort of evidence that can be gleaned from, for example, a reputable publication as to used car prices. Indeed, I, for my part, would strongly wish to discourage the notion that expert evidence, as such, is necessary or desirable in small claims arbitrations of this kind in relation to common items.)'

Further:

'The case was conducted on the assumption that the question of the valuation of the car was a proper matter for the calling in person of expert evidence on both sides. I question that assumption on the grounds of proportionality.'

The court referred to CPR 27.5 and to the rule that 'No expert may give evidence, whether written or oral, at a hearing without the permission of the court'.

'I would say nothing to encourage the grant of such a permission in a case such as this for reasons of proportionality. There are published guides available in newsagents and used in the trade that give some indication as to the market price of secondhand cars which judges may find helpful. I suggest that, in the ordinary case, such guides would give better evidential value for money than the expensive calling of two live experts.'

Owners of the ship Pelopidas and Owners of the ship TRSL Concord (1999)

In a shipping collision case, the judge made a number of observations about the role of expert evidence in Admiralty cases. Of more general application was the observation that a sense of proportion must be maintained in efforts to reduce disagreement between experts on non-essential matters, where precision and therefore absolute unanimity are difficult to achieve:

'It is important that a degree of discipline is maintained as regards expert evidence. Where the resolution of the difference of opinion between the experts cannot have any material influence on the outcome of the action, it is incumbent on the parties to avoid incurring the costs of trying to achieve that resolution.'

Kranidiotes v Paschali (2001)

In a dispute over control of a company, the judge directed the appointment of a single joint expert (SJE) to report on the value of the company and shareholdings in it. The order set a maximum overall fee of £10,000, based on the sums in dispute. The Deloitte & Touche SJE appointed realised on investigation that he could not deal with the matters raised in submissions within this limit and notified the court accordingly. The court terminated the SJE's appointment and the appellant appealed against this decision. The Court of Appeal dismissed the appeal:

> '... it is quite clear that this court will not interfere with a case management decision, such as the one under consideration in this case, unless it considers that the judge has exceeded the generous ambit within which a reasonable disagreement is possible.

> In the present case the judge had to and did have in mind the need for a proportionate approach. That is quite clear from the reasons that he gave. He limited the new expert to an initial budget of £10,000.

> ... the amount of money in issue did not warrant a payment of very substantial costs ... I believe it fell well within the ambit of his discretion to decide as he did'.

4

Court powers and single joint experts

CPR 35.4 gives the court powers to restrict expert evidence generally and CPR 35.7 and 35.8 give powers to direct the appointment and instruction of a single joint expert (SJE).

This section contains cases governing the restriction or exclusion of expert evidence and particularly the use of SJEs. It is divided into two parts:

4.1 Courts' powers to allow or exclude expert evidence
4.2 Courts' powers in relation to single joint experts

4.1 COURTS' POWERS TO ALLOW OR EXCLUDE EXPERT EVIDENCE

While under CPR 35.9 the court has power to direct a party to provide information, it cannot force a party to submit a report on an issue where no expert evidence is to be adduced: *Derby & Co Ltd v Weldon*. The court does have the power to issue a witness summons ('subpoena' in the pre-CPR cases) but will only do so in appropriate cases. It would not be appropriate to issue a witness summons to compel the attendance of an expert whose fees a party could no longer afford: *Brown v Bennett*; nor where the holder of a vital public office would be kept from his duty: *Society of Lloyd's v Clementson*. The *Society of Lloyd's* case contains guidance from the Court of Appeal on factors to be taken into account in exercising the court's discretion to compel attendance of an expert witness.

The fact that the parties themselves agree that an expert should be called will not automatically secure his appointment: in *Stevens v Gullis* the court refused to sanction a consent order for a surveyor witness previously debarred as unsatisfactory.

Many of the cases dealing with exclusion of experts and their evidence arise from time difficulties. They provide salutary warning that the ability to call experts may be lost if time limits are not met. In *Beachley Property v Edgar* and *Dew Pitchmastic plc v Birse Construction Ltd*, disorganisation of the parties and/or their legal advisers led to the courts refusing to grant extension of time, although *Mortgage Corporation Ltd v Sandoes* set out guidelines which are seen as something of an amelioration of this harshness (and which have been followed since the CPR were introduced). Legal teams have also got into difficulty with the unavailability of expert witnesses, and generally speaking the courts are unsympathetic to this as a ground for granting an extension: *Rollinson v Kimberley Clark Ltd*. Unavailability without explanation is especially unlikely to command support: *Simon Andrew Matthews v Tarmac Bricks and Tiles Ltd*.

The court was held to have an inherent jurisdiction to refuse an order where the other party's position would be jeopardised: *Winchester Cigarette Machinery Ltd v Payne*.

Derby & Co Ltd v Weldon (No 9) (1990)

In a case in which conspiracy to defraud purchasers by misstating the value of a company was alleged by the claimants, the claimants argued that the court could compel the defendants to submit expert accountancy evidence. The defendants had indicated that they would not call such evidence. The court held that it could not order a party to submit an expert's report on an issue on which it did not intend to adduce any expert evidence.

Brown v Bennett (2002)

The court set aside a witness summons issued against an expert witness by the claimants in an action, who could no longer afford to pay her fees. The court accepted the proposition in *Phipson on Evidence* (15th edn, 2001) paras 37–49 that 'an unwilling expert witness will, save in an exceptional case, be released from the operation of a subpoena'. The court was not persuaded that the facts of the case were 'exceptional'; the claimants were simply trying to avoid paying the fees of the expert witness by seeking an order to compel her attendance.

Society of Lloyd's v Clementson (No 2) (1996)

The Court of Appeal allowed an appeal by the Chairman of Lloyd's against a subpoena served on him by the defendant underwriter in an action by Lloyd's to recover sums paid from the Lloyd's central fund to discharge the defendant's liabilities. The court said that a judge had a discretion whether to compel persons to appear as an expert witness against their will. Factors to be taken into account in exercising that discretion included:

(1) that a court is prima facie entitled to every man's evidence, whether of fact or opinion;
(2) whether the expert has some connection with the case in question;
(3) whether the expert is willing to come, provided that his image is protected by the issue of a subpoena;
(4) whether attendance at court will disrupt or impede other important work that he has to do; and
(5) whether another expert of equal calibre is available.

In these circumstances, the court could not accept that there was no other means for the defendants to obtain expert evidence about the workings of Lloyd's, although maybe more than one expert would be required. It was also a powerful point that the Chairman of Lloyd's was an important office holder, who should not be required to spend days in court giving evidence, and time preparing it, unless that was essential.

Stevens v Gullis (1999)

In an action by the claimant builder against the defendant client, the client's only expert failed to respond to a memorandum of agreement prepared by the experts and was eventually debarred from being called as an expert witness. There were also third party proceedings by the client against his architect under CPR Part 20. The judge decided that, as there was now no expert evidence available in the third party proceedings, they should be discontinued. The claimant and the client agreed that the expert debarred by the judge should be used as a witness of fact, the client having consulted a new expert. However, the Court of Appeal refused to sanction a consent order to this effect. Their view was that this would impose on the judge an expert who did not understand his obligations to the court.

Beachley Property Ltd v Edgar (1996)

In a claim for breach of covenant of a lease, the claimant failed to serve witness statements for several key witnesses on time and then sought leave for late service a fortnight before trial. The court had to consider whether changes of personnel in a solicitor's office would constitute a justification for late service and whether an argument that no prejudice had been caused by the delay should necessarily prevail.

Lord Woolf, giving judgment against the background of the introduction of his reforms in the CPR, rejected the appeal against the exclusion of the reports:

> 'The explanation for the witness statements being served so late, and for the application being made at the relatively last moment for leave for those witnesses' evidence to be adduced at the hearing, is apparently that there was a change in the [claimant's] solicitors' office so that the same person was not dealing with the case throughout. I would emphasise that I regard that as no explanation or excuse whatsoever for the non-compliance with directions with regard to witness statements ...'

Further:

> 'It was submitted [for the appellant] that unless there was some evidence of prejudice on their part which could be shown by the defendant, in these circumstances the court has no alternative but to allow the calling of the evidence ... I would like to make it absolutely clear that I do not accept that submission. The very reason why the order is drafted in the terms that it is, is to ensure that unless there are circumstances which justify the court exercising discretion in favour of the party in default, that discretion will not be exercised and the party will be deprived of the evidence.'

Dew Pitchmastic plc v Birse Construction Ltd (2000)

Where the defendants in a construction dispute failed, without satisfactory reason, to adhere to the timetable for instruction of experts – failing to instruct them in time and failing to get them to meet their obligations in time – the court would have to consider whether the position of the claimants would be jeopardised. The defendants' defaults in this case were so serious that there was a real danger that, by the time of the trial, the claimants would not know the case they had to meet.

Accordingly, no further extension of time would be granted to the defendants and permission to call expert witnesses would be refused: 'A party cannot be allowed to get away with thinking that it can comply with the timetable as and when it is ready to do so.'

Mortgage Corporation Ltd v Sandoes (1996)

The claimant appealed against being refused an extension of time for exchange of witness statements and experts' reports in a professional negligence claim. The Court of Appeal, allowing the appeal, set out guidance to courts on adherence to time limits (this goes beyond expert witness issues).

The court described these guidelines as issued by agreement with the Master of the Rolls and the Vice Chancellor:

'1. Time requirements laid down by the Rules and directions given by the Court are not merely targets to be attempted; they are rules to be observed.
2. At the same time the overriding principle is that justice must be done.
3. Litigants are entitled to have their cases resolved with reasonable expedition. Non-compliance with time limits can cause prejudice to one or more of the parties to the litigation.
4. In addition the vacation or adjournment of the date of trial prejudices other litigants and disrupts the administration of justice.
5. Extensions of time which involve the vacation or adjournment of trial dates should therefore be granted only as a last resort.

6. Where time limits have not been complied with, the parties should co-operate in reaching an agreement as to new time limits which will not involve the date of trial being postponed.
7. If they reach such an agreement they can ordinarily expect the court to give effect to that agreement at the trial and it is not necessary to make a separate application solely for this purpose.
8. The court will not look with favour on a party who seeks only to take tactical advantage from the failure of another party to comply with time limits.
9. In the absence of an agreement as to a new timetable, an application should be made promptly to the court for directions.
10. In considering whether to grant an extension of time to a party who is in default, the court will look at all the circumstances of the case including the considerations identified above.'

Note: The above case is described by the editors of CILL as representing 'some softening' of *Beachley Property v Edgar*.

Rollinson v Kimberley Clark Ltd (1999)

The Court of Appeal dismissed Kimberley Clark's appeal against a judge's refusal to vacate a court hearing date for trial of a personal injury claim by one of the company's employees. The defendant's application came in February 1999 to vacate a June 1999 trial date, due to the unavailability of its second medical expert witness. The court held that:

'... if it ever was acceptable ... it is certainly no longer acceptable when a trial date is bound to be fairly imminent, for a solicitor to seek to instruct an expert witness without checking and discovering his availability, or proceed to instruct him when there is no reasonable prospect of his being available for another year. The check having been made and the experts' availability in the near future being in doubt, then a different expert should be instructed'.

Simon Andrew Matthews v Tarmac Bricks and Tiles Ltd (2000)

In a personal injury case, counsel for the defendants objected to a date fixed for trial by the judge at the Pre-Trial Review, because it was one of a list of dates on which the defendants' medical expert witnesses would not be available. The judge refused to change the trial date and the defendants appealed. The Court of Appeal upheld the judge's decision:

> 'The approach which was being adopted by the lawyers before the judge was wholly inappropriate. They were adopting what in the past has been an approach which has been too frequently adopted. They were regarding it as the responsibility of the court to defer the hearing to a date which could, with convenience, be met by the doctors.'

Further:

> 'The parties cannot always expect the courts to meet their convenience … If there is no agreement as to the dates which are acceptable to the court, the lawyers for the parties must be in a position to give the reasons why certain dates are not convenient to doctors.'

Winchester Cigarette Machinery Ltd v Payne (1993)

The Court of Appeal dismissed an appeal by the defendants against a judge's order debarring them from calling experts at a late stage in proceedings. The defendants sought to call experts in an action due to be heard three weeks later in a hearing scheduled for 15 days. The court held that the judge had been correct to refuse leave to call the experts so late, in circumstances where prejudice to the claimants would result, because of the need to seek an adjournment to deal with the changed situation. The court retains an inherent discretion to refuse an order where the other party's position would be jeopardised.

4.2 COURTS' POWERS IN RELATION TO SINGLE JOINT EXPERTS

Under CPR 35.7, the court may direct that evidence is given by one expert only, either to be agreed between the parties or selected by the court.

The courts have tried to uphold this principle, especially where it is supported by proportionality to cost: *Layland v Fairview Homes plc*. Where it has been abrogated in smaller cases, this has occasioned judicial criticism: *Roadrunner Properties Ltd v Dean*. However, there is no *presumption* in CPR 35.7 in favour of a SJE appointment: *Oxley v Penwarden*. And in more complex cases the courts have found it necessary to be flexible and to accommodate demands, in certain situations, for the parties to have their own experts. In *Simms v Birmingham Health Authority*, this was because it was premature to make a SJE appointment; the parties needed their own experts at the outset. But in *Daniels v Walker* and *Cosgrove v Pattison* the courts have set out guidance on factors to be taken into account in deciding applications by parties to call their own experts where a SJE has been appointed, guidance applied in *Austen v Oxford City Council*.

The courts are also evolving, of necessity, rules governing the management of SJEs in such matters as meetings: *Peet v Mid-Kent Healthcare NHS Trust* and *Smith v Stephens*; instructions: *Yorke v Katra* in Section 6.1; and fees: *Kranidiotes v Paschali* in Section 3.3.

Layland v Fairview Homes plc (2003)

This is one of the earliest reported decisions on the court's power to appoint SJEs under CPR 36.7. The court noted that such an appointment will be particularly attractive in low value claims where the issue for expert evidence is easy to identify. The case concerned a claim by purchasers of a flat against the developers and local planning authority for damages allegedly caused by diminution in value of their flat after the authority granted itself planning permission for a waste disposal plant nearby.

The first instance judge had been entitled to reject two reports produced by the claimants disagreeing with that of the SJE, since these were produced late and offered no solid evidence not taken into account by the SJE. The court has discretion as to whether to allow parties to call their own experts; here, where the claim was small and the contribution of the new experts was dubious, it would be disallowed. Apart from this, 'the Court will normally permit a party to call his own expert, if he has reasonable grounds for wishing to take that course'. However, on appeal, the judge had been wrong to strike out the claim; there was a realistic possibility of diminution in value which could only be tested at trial by cross-examination of the SJE.

Roadrunner Properties Ltd v Dean (2004)

In a party wall dispute, where works had been carried out without notice, the dispute centred upon the issue of causation and the conflict of evidence called. The Court of Appeal took the opportunity to comment on the deployment of expert witnesses in a claim of £6,707. The court noted that at first a district judge had ordered that expert evidence should be limited to a SJE, but that this order had been revoked when the parties were unable to agree on an acceptable appointment.

'It is not simply with the advantage of hindsight that one can say that this was not a case in which more than a single jointly instructed expert should have been allowed to give evidence. It was manifest from the pleaded issues that all that was required was a knowledgeable account of the possible causes of the observed damage. It would then have been for the judge to decide which was the more (or, if more than two, the most) probable ... [The court referred to Rule 35.7 of the Civil Procedure Rules.] This was, in my judgment, a paradigm case for the exercise of the power of the court to break the deadlock by naming its own expert or by providing for a single expert to be otherwise nominated. A single expert was all that was needed to tabulate the possible causes of the damage.'

Oxley v Penwarden (2001)

In a medical negligence case, in a case management conference which the judge conducted by telephone, he stated his view that the parties should agree a SJE vascular surgeon on the issue of causation. Should the parties fail to agree, the court would take on the appointment of the SJE itself. Neither side was content with this approach.

The Court of Appeal called attention to the note attached to CPR 35.7:

'There is no presumption in favour of the appointment of a single joint expert. The object is to do away with the calling of multiple experts where, given the nature of the issue over which the parties are at odds, that is not justified.'

The court referred to the general advantages of SJEs mentioned in the note 'of reducing costs and delay and [to] strengthen the impartial role of experts'.

However, in a case like this 'it was necessary for the parties to have the opportunity of investigating causation through an expert of their own choice and, further, to have the opportunity of calling that evidence before the court'. If the parties could not then agree, the burden would be cast upon the court and the judge's choice might well decide an essential question in the case without the opportunity of challenge.

Simms v Birmingham Health Authority (2001)

In a medical negligence case, it was held that the judge had acted prematurely in ordering the parties to appoint a named SJE before the parties had pleaded their respective cases. Each side should be entitled to have its own expert at this stage. While the time might come later for a SJE appointment, until the issues were before the court, it would be premature to make an order as to what experts should be called or to ascertain what duplication existed between them.

Daniels v Walker (2000)

In a personal injury case, the court had to consider whether the defendant should be allowed to have the injured claimant examined by its own expert, as well as by a jointly-instructed occupational therapist. The defendant was unhappy with the claimant's instructions to the occupational therapist. Lord Woolf MR held that:

'Where the parties have sensibly agreed to instruct an expert, it is obviously preferable that the form of instructions should be agreed if possible. Failing agreement, it is perfectly proper for either separate instructions to be given by one of the parties or for supplementary instructions to be given by one of the parties.'

Further:

'In the majority of cases, the sensible approach will not be to ask the court straight away to allow the dissatisfied party to call a second expert. In many cases it would be wrong to make a decision until one is in a position to consider the situation in the round.'

However, in this case, where there was a substantial amount of money involved and where no undue distress would be caused by a further examination, a further examination and report should have been allowed.

If there is disagreement on the report of a SJE, questions could be put to the SJE or a party could seek to have its own report. The court will have to decide on what evidence is to be called if one or both parties have their own expert. Oral evidence by them in court will be 'a last resort', because of the cost, and only after the experts have met to attempt to reach agreement.

Cosgrove v Pattison (2001)

In a neighbour dispute where a SJE had been appointed pursuant to CPR 35.8, the defendants sought permission to call their own expert. Overturning the refusal of the district judge to allow this, the court set out the factors to be considered when deciding such an application:

'... although it would be wrong to pretend that this is an exhaustive list, the factors to be taken into account when considering an application to permit a further expert to be called are these. First, the nature of the issue or issues; secondly, the number of issues between the parties; thirdly, the reason the new expert is wanted; fourthly, the amount at stake and, if it is not purely money, the nature of the issues at stake and their importance; fifthly, the effect of permitting one party to call further expert evidence on the conduct of the trial; sixthly, the delay, if any, in making the application; seventhly, any delay that the instructing and calling of the new expert will cause; eighthly, any special features of the case; and finally, and in a sense all embracing, the overall justice to the parties in the context of the litigation'.

See *Daniels v Walker*, applied in the above case.

Austen v Oxford City Council (2002)

In a personal injury action, an order for a SJE to give psychiatric evidence was made by the district judge. The claimant's solicitors agreed to the defendants' proposal of their own expert as SJE and, when a highly unfavourable report was delivered, the claimant's solicitors accepted it and proceeded with the claim, taking the view that the report would only be given limited weight – a view which the judge described as 'bizarre'. The judge then refused leave for the SJE to be cross-examined. The claimant appealed.

The court referred to *Daniels v Walker* as authority for the proposition that a party dissatisfied with the report of a SJE can ask the court for permission to instruct and call another expert; and to *Peet v Mid Kent Healthcare NHS* to the effect that if a SJE is called to give oral evidence, both parties should have the opportunity to cross-examine the SJE. In this situation:

> 'How far the cross-examination would have been permitted would have been for the trial judge who had a discretion to allow it in the first place ... The cross-examination would have been likely to be sufficient to persuade the Judge to resile from the black and white view he had obviously formed ... His decision deprived the claimant of that limited opportunity.'

Peet v Mid-Kent Healthcare NHS Trust (2002)

Where the parties in a medical negligence case had instructed a SJE, it was not permissible for one party to meet the SJE in the absence of the other party, unless the other party gave prior written consent. The claimants' solicitors had requested a meeting with the SJE without the presence of the defendant health authority's solicitors, which they claimed would inhibit and traumatise the claimants.

Lord Woolf rejected this submission:

> '... the idea of having an experts' conference including lawyers without there being a representative of the defendant present, as was suggested by the claimant's solicitors, in my judgment is inconsistent with the whole concept of the single expert.
>
> The framework to which I have made reference is designed to ensure an open process so that both sides know exactly what information is placed before the single expert. It would be totally inconsistent with the whole of that structure to allow one party to conduct a conference where the evidence of the experts is in effect tested in the course of discussions which take place with that expert. I emphasise that what I have just said does not prevent one expert from communicating with another expert in order to obtain any information which that expert requires to include in his or her report'.

See *Smith v Stephens* on a similar point.

Smith v Stephens (2001)

Even though CPR Part 35 did not confer an express power on a court to prevent meetings, the court has power under its inherent jurisdiction to issue an order restraining a meeting in breach of the overriding objectives of CPR Part 35. Here the claimant's solicitor arranged a meeting with seven SJEs appointed to take place without the defendant or his advisors being present.

Notwithstanding the normal right of a party to interview witnesses as part of its preparation for trial, where the court has directed the instruction of a SJE it will be inconsistent with that direction and the overriding objective of the CPR for one side secretly to ascertain the views of the expert. Where, as here, the parties could not agree on a meeting with the SJE, it would be necessary to fall back on the submission of written questions and the provision of written answers.

See *Peet v Mid-Kent Healthcare NHS Trust* on a similar point.

5
Pre-hearing matters

This section contains cases dealing with two pre-hearing matters, namely the related issues of the following:

5.1 Disclosure, confidentiality and privilege
5.2 Meetings and agreements between expert witnesses

5.1 DISCLOSURE, CONFIDENTIALITY AND PRIVILEGE

In addition to the wider CPR powers relating to disclosure under Part 31, the court has power under CPR 35.9 to direct a party to provide information to the other party. None of these powers destroy the basic concepts of confidentiality and privilege attaching to communications between parties and their legal/professional advisers. This privilege survived a challenge based on allegation of joint instruction: *Carlton v Townsend*; and on the argument of entitlement to see how an expert's view had 'developed' between first report and final report. The position of privilege is, of course, more complex where an expert's report is mistakenly sent to the other side: *Webster v James Chapman & Co and Kenning v Eve Construction*. A crucial question is often the scope of the material covered by privilege: in *Clough v Tameside and Glossop Health Authority*, a report by another specialist and related communications; and in *Lucas v Barking Havering & Redbridge NHS Trust*, material supplied by the instructing party to the expert. In *West Midlands Passenger Transport Executive v Singh*, the disclosure of statistical material incorporated into an expert's report was ordered; and in *London & Leeds Estates Ltd v Paribas Ltd (No 2)* a landlord's expert witness was held to be obliged to disclose evidence of statements as to market conditions made in an earlier arbitration which were inconsistent with those he was now putting forward.

In the specific situation where a party is applying for leave to appoint a second expert, the court may require disclosure of the first expert's report: *Beck v Ministry of Defence* and *Hajigeorglou v Vasiliou*.

The normal rules of discovery apply to parties acting as experts, here engineers defending a professional negligence claim, giving expert evidence on their own behalf: *Shell Pensions Trust v Pell Frischmann & Partners.*

Carlton v Townsend (2001)

In a personal injury case, and following the Pre-Action Protocol for Personal Injury Claims, the claimant's solicitors informed the defendant's insurers that they intended to instruct one of three named orthopaedic surgeons as expert witnesses. The insurers objected to one and another was instructed. The defendant's insurers argued that the instructions to the expert were to be on a joint instruction basis and they expected simultaneous access to the report. In the High Court, the judge had concluded that the report was privileged because only the claimant had instructed the expert. The Court of Appeal held that, just because the defendant's insurers had not objected to the expert in question, this did not make him a single joint expert (SJE). The court could not override the privilege between the expert and the solicitors instructing him.

Webster v James Chapman & Co (1989)

In an industrial injury case, a report by the employee's consulting engineer expert was accidentally sent to the employers' solicitors. It contained certain findings adverse to the employee's case. The employee's solicitors sought the return of the report and an undertaking that it would not be used. A subsequent report, much more favourable to the employee, was subsequently submitted to be relied upon at trial. The court rejected the argument that the employers should not be allowed to use the first report:

> 'The expert will be amenable to cross-examination. He is likely to be asked his opinion on causation and contributory negligence. He may say that he has previously expressed an opinion on those matters. He may deny it. Whichever way it goes, it seems to me that the conduct of the defendant's case would be seriously embarrassed if the defendant and its legal advisers were

not able to make use of their knowledge of the contents of the original report, knowledge that has come into their possession through no fault of theirs ... if there is an explanation which the expert can give of the difference between the reports, so be it, he can give it. If there is no explanation he can give, it does not seem to me that to allow that to become apparent would represent injustice.'

Kenning v Eve Construction Ltd (1989)

A personal injury case was brought against the defendant employers, who commissioned a report from an engineer as expert. The engineer's report, dealing with the allegations of negligence, was, however, accompanied by a letter, suggesting ways in which the defendants might have been negligent. The letter was mistakenly sent to the claimant's solicitors, who sought leave to amend the pleadings to include the new grounds of negligence thus revealed. The defendants argued that the claimant should be restrained from using the letter. The court held that, although the expert's letter was privileged, the whole substance of his evidence would have to be disclosed if the defendants decided to call him, which was their choice.

'If an expert witness is approached by a solicitor on behalf of his client and overall the expert's view is unfavourable to the merits of the case that he is having to consider, the solicitor has a choice. He can either call him (in which case, as it seems to me, he ought to be prepared to disclose his evidence with both the favourable and unfavourable parts contained) or he does not call him and seeks another expert's opinion which may be more favourable.'

Further:

'... the solicitor's choice is simple. He must make up his mind whether he wishes to rely upon that expert, having balanced the good parts of the report against the bad parts. If he decides that on balance the expert if worth calling, then he must call him on the basis of all the evidence that he can give, not merely the evidence that he can give under examination-in-chief, taking the good with the bad together'.

Clough v Tameside and Glossop Health Authority (1998)

In a medical negligence case, the defendant health authority sought to resist an application by the claimant's lawyers for an order that they should produce a psychiatric report and related communications used by the defendants' medical expert witness. The defendants argued that, while they had served their medical expert's report, the other material remained privileged. The court rejected the defendants' arguments: where an expert witness refers in his report to material supplied to him by his instructing solicitor as part of the background information on which the report is based, the privilege attaching to that information is the same as attaches to the report itself, and is therefore waived when it is served.

> 'If an expert has discounted some evidence supplied to him, he may, at the conclusion of the case, be held wrong to have done so and his opinion may thereby be invalidated. Equally, he may have assumed an incorrect significance for a particular piece of material. It is only by proper and full disclosure to all parties that an expert's opinion can be tested in court: in order to ascertain whether all appropriate information was supplied and how the expert dealt with it. It is not for one party to keep their cards face down on the table so that the other party does not know the full extent of information supplied. Fairness dictates that a party should not be forced to meet a case pleaded or an expert opinion on the basis of the documents he cannot see.'

But see also *Lucas v Barking, Havering and Redbridge Hospital NHS Trust.*

Lucas v Barking, Havering & Redbridge NHS Trust (2004)

In the claimant's action against the defendant health authority for personal injury, a dispute arose as to whether material supplied to an expert by an instructing party formed part of the expert's 'instructions' for the purposes of CPR 35.10(3). The Court of Appeal held that 'Material supplied by the instructing party as the basis on which the expert is being asked to advise should ... be considered as part of the instructions'. The court would not under CPR 35.10(4) order disclosure or permit questioning unless satisfied that there are reasonable grounds to consider the statement of instructions under CPR 35.10(3) to be inaccurate or incomplete. There was no basis to assert that and so disclosure would be refused.

Note: *Clough v Tameside and Glossop HA* reconsidered.

West Midlands Passenger Transport Executive v Singh (1988)

In an employment case where race discrimination was alleged against the Transport Executive, the Court of Appeal upheld an order by the industrial tribunal for discovery of certain statistical evidence. The test was stated to be that the material must be relevant and necessary for the fair disposal of the case and discovery must not be oppressive to either party. These requirements for discovery of the material on which a party's evidence is based are not confined to cases of this kind.

London & Leeds Estates Ltd v Paribas Ltd (No 2) (1995)

In an arbitration of a rent review dispute, the tenant sought leave for disclosure of proofs of evidence given by the landlords' expert witness in earlier separate arbitrations, which the tenant argued contained statements by the experts inconsistent with the evidence as to market conditions they were now giving. The court rejected the contrary argument that these were covered by privilege, so that the experts could not be cross-examined on them:

> 'If a witness were proved to have expressed himself in a materially different sense when acting for different sides, that would be a factor which should be brought out in the interests of individual litigants involved and in the public interest.'

So the evidence would have to be disclosed, although this did not apply to evidence given in an unrelated arbitration by the experts; the defendants' desire to refer to this was described as no more than a 'fishing expedition'.

Beck v Ministry of Defence (2003)

In a personal injury case, where the claimant had been examined by the defendants' expert, the defendants sought leave to instruct a new expert because they were dissatisfied with his conclusions. The Court of Appeal held that the first expert's report would have to be disclosed in such circumstances.

> 'Once the judge has decided to allow a new expert to be instructed, there is no reason not to disclose the discarded expert's report and every reason to disclose it. The disclosure of the original report should be a condition of the defendant being allowed to instruct a new expert ...'

Hajigeorglou v Vasiliou (2005)

In a landlord and tenant dispute, the court granted permission for the parties to instruct one expert witness each on restaurant valuation. The landlords sought to rely on the evidence of a second expert witness. The judge, following *Beck v Ministry of Defence*, held that the landlords required permission to appoint a second expert but that the court would grant it provided the first expert's report was disclosed to the tenant. However, the Court of Appeal upheld the landlords' appeal. Whereas in *Beck* the order had identified the two experts, so that their reports should be disclosed even if they were not relied upon, here the order deliberately only identified the area of expertise. The landlords could therefore rely upon another expert from that area if they chose.

See *Beck v Ministry of Defence*.

Shell Pensions Trust Ltd v Pell Frischmann & Partners (1986)

In a professional negligence action brought by the claimant owners against their consultant engineers, the engineers proposed to give expert evidence on their own behalf. The owners sought discovery of the evidence on which the engineers intended to rely. The court held that a defendant who wishes to give expert evidence on his own behalf to rebut allegations of professional negligence (for example) must disclose the evidence to be relied upon under normal principles of discovery, just as an ordinary expert witness would have to do.

'... the Court had power in this case to direct that the substance of any expert evidence which the defendant consultant engineers intend to give on their behalf should be disclosed in the form of written reports ... The reports should disclose the opinion evidence on which the defendants wish to rely'.

5.2 MEETINGS AND AGREEMENTS BETWEEN EXPERT WITNESSES

The attitude of the law generally, and of the CPR in particular, is to encourage meetings and, where possible, agreements between experts, in the interests of narrowing areas of dispute and saving time and money. CPR 35.12(1) to 35.12(4) contain powers by which the court may direct discussions between experts. General encouragement to meet on site to try to agree the 'irreducible and stubborn facts' goes back to *Graigola Merthyr Co Ltd v Swansea Corporation* but is equally evident post-CPR in *Hubbard v Lambeth Southwark and Lewisham Health Authority*, where the Court of Appeal saw scope for experts to narrow issues to be determined at trial even in very complex cases, indeed 'in almost every case'. There would have to be strong grounds to rebut this presumption, and objection by one party would not normally be enough.

Special care is given by the courts to meetings with SJEs, however. The court will be anxious to avoid compromising the essential fairness of the joint appointment which would arise from meetings between the SJE and one party and its advisers: *Peet v Mid-Kent Healthcare Trust* and *Smith v Stephens*.

So far as agreement is concerned, expert witnesses do not normally possess 'implied' or 'ostensible' authority to agree facts orally or in any way other than a joint report: *Carnell Computer Technology Ltd v Unipart Group Ltd*; although the parties can give their experts such authority: *Richard Roberts Holdings Ltd v Douglas Smith Stimson Partnership (No 2)*.

CPR 35.12(5) states that agreements reached between the experts do not bind the parties unless the parties agree to be bound and this has been applied in *Robin Ellis Ltd v Malwright* and *Britannia Zinc Ltd v Connect South West Ltd.*

Where there is an agreement between the experts as to facts, the court should not normally look behind that agreement: *Stringfellow v Blyth* in Section 7.2.

Graigola Merthyr Co Ltd v Swansea Corporation (1928)

Mine owners sought an injunction to prevent the local authority filling its reservoir, alleging that it would flood their adjacent mine-shafts. The court made a number of observations on the duties of expert witnesses in preparing to give evidence for complex technical disputes to avoid waste of time and money.

'Of late years cases involving expert evidence appear to have increased in number and in length. Having regard to the complexity of modern life and the widened field over which science ranges, this is perhaps inevitable, but the overloading of these cases in the preparation of them is becoming not infrequent. Long cases produce evils; they place the parties with the lesser resources at a grave disadvantage, and they delay the course of the general business of the Courts and thereby inflict serious hardship on other litigants. In every case of this kind there are generally many "irreducible and stubborn facts" upon which agreement between experts should be possible, and in my judgment the expert advisers of the parties, whether legal or scientific, are under a special duty to the Court in the preparation of such a case to limit in every possible way the contentious matters of fact to be dealt with at the hearing ... Experts on both sides paid numerous visits to the *locus in quo*, both underground and on the surface, but the experts never met on the spot to see whether ... they could not reach a measure of accord ...'

Further:

'... all concerned in litigation of this class must in future in the preparation of their cases more closely address their minds to restricting the area of dispute'.

Hubbard v Lambeth Southwark & Lewisham Health Authority (2001)

In a medical negligence case, the claimants objected to an order by the master at a case management conference that the respective experts should meet to discuss matters of practice and treatment with a view to an agreement. The claimants appealed from the order, arguing that their experts should not be forced to meet with the defendants' expert who was renowned as pre-eminent in the field. The Court of Appeal dismissed the appeal:

> '... in almost every case experts are able to narrow the issues to be determined at trial even in very complex cases. The time and cost benefit which flows from this is obvious. There are of course cases where an experts' meeting would serve no purpose, in which case no order should be made. But, even if both parties object to a meeting, the court is not prevented from making an order and should do so if it thinks that something will come of it. I see nothing wrong with a general approach that an order for such discussions to take place will usually be made where there has been an exchange of expert reports.

> The mere objection by one party will not be sufficient. Some very good reason for not having a meeting would have to be shown ... it seems to me that the real fear is that at this meeting [the claimants' experts] might be tempted to sell their clients down the river. I do not think that is a good reason'.

Peet v Mid-Kent Healthcare NHS Trust (2002)

Where the parties in a medical negligence case had instructed a SJE, it was not permissible for one party to meet the SJE in the absence of the other party, unless the other party gave prior written consent. The claimants' solicitors had requested a meeting with the SJE without the presence of the defendant health authority's solicitors, which they claimed would inhibit and traumatise the claimants.

Lord Woolf rejected this submission:

> '... the idea of having an experts' conference including lawyers without there being a representative of the

defendant present, as was suggested by the claimant's solicitors, in my judgment is inconsistent with the whole concept of the single expert.

The framework to which I have made reference is designed to ensure an open process so that both sides know exactly what information is placed before the single expert. It would be totally inconsistent with the whole of that structure to allow one party to conduct a conference where the evidence of the experts is in effect tested in the course of discussions which take place with that expert. I emphasise that what I have just said does not prevent one expert from communicating with another expert in order to obtain any information which that expert requires to include in his or her report'.

See *Smith v Stephens* on a similar point.

Smith v Stephens (2001)

Even though CPR Part 35 did not confer an express power on a court to prevent meetings, the court has power under its inherent jurisdiction to issue an order restraining a meeting in breach of the overriding objectives of CPR Part 35. Here the claimant's solicitor arranged a meeting with seven appointed SJEs to take place without the defendant or his advisors being present.

Notwithstanding the normal right of a party to interview witnesses as part of its preparation for trial, where the court has directed the instruction of a SJE, it will be inconsistent with that direction and the overriding objective of the CPR for one side secretly to ascertain the views of the expert. Where, as here, the parties could not agree on a meeting with the SJE, it would be necessary to fall back on the submission of written questions and the provision of written answers.

See *Peet v Mid-Kent Healthcare NHS Trust* on a similar point.

Carnell Computer Technology Ltd v Unipart Group Ltd (1988)

An expert witness has no 'implied' or 'ostensible' authority to agree facts orally or in any form other than a joint report.

However, the parties can give the experts such authority: see *Richard Roberts Holdings v Douglas Smith Stimson Partnership (No 2)*.

Richard Roberts Holdings Ltd v Douglas Smith Stimson Partnership (No 2) (1989)

A document produced by the parties' respective expert witnesses recording the substance of their agreement could constitute an agreement binding on both parties, although it would not automatically do so. Although the discussions between the experts were themselves 'without prejudice', where the parties held out their experts as having authority to reach agreement within the scope of those discussions, they could do so. The court observed that in any event, once the experts had agreed, neither could give evidence contrary to the agreement and the court would be unlikely to allow new experts to be called so late in proceedings.

Note that such authority would not be automatic: See *Carnell Computer Technology v Unipart Group Ltd.*

Robin Ellis Ltd v Malwright (1999)

The court having ordered the parties' experts in a construction dispute to meet without prejudice to narrow and agree facts, the experts produced a Joint Statement. The court held that:

> 'The Joint Statement which the experts were ordered to produce is a document produced for the Court to assist the Court in case management of the litigation and also in management of the conduct of the trial. It is not a document which one party (or both parties) can withhold from the Court by a claim of privilege.'

Conversely, the product of the discussions is not binding on the parties; it 'may be referred to as a compromise but it is not a compromise in the sense of a compromise agreement binding on the parties'.

Britannia Zinc Ltd v Connect South West Ltd (2002)

In a dispute between loss adjuster experts for the respective parties regarding repair of damage to a cable, an agreement was reached between them as to the loss suffered. Connect argued that it was not bound by that agreement.

CPR 35.12(5) provides that, in relation to discussions between experts pursuant to a direction of the court, 'where experts reach agreement on an issue during their discussion, the agreement shall not bind the parties unless the parties expressly agree to be bound by the agreement'.

It was suggested in argument that implied authority to agree existed, but the judge held that:

> '... it is plain from the terms of CPR 35.12(5) that implied authority is not sufficient to enable a party's expert witness to bind it by any agreement which he might make with an expert acting on behalf of an opposite party'.

6
The expert witness's report

This section deals with aspects of the evidence provided by the expert witness. Under CPR 35.5 there is a general requirement for expert evidence to be given in a written report and this form is usual even where, as before arbitration tribunals, there is no equivalent mandatory requirement.

The section is divided into three parts:

6.1 Instructions to the expert witness
6.2 The report and the evidence it contains
6.3 Examination and cross-examination on the report

6.1 INSTRUCTIONS TO THE EXPERT WITNESS

Prior to the CPR, there was concern to avoid a situation where an expert witness instructed by one side was subsequently instructed by the other, creating a potential conflict of interest, although it was said that 'There is no property in an expert witness': *Harmony Shipping Co v Saudi Europe Line Ltd (The Good Helm)*. Since the introduction of the single joint expert (SJE), in particular, new considerations have arisen in the instruction of the expert witness. By definition, of course, there is no conflict of interest in a SJE being instructed by both parties. This need not only mean joint instruction, however. CPR 35.8(1) contemplates the possibility that 'each instructing party may give instructions to the expert': *Yorke v Katra*. The fact that one party does not object to the other instructing the expert does not mean that this is a joint instruction basis: *Carlton v Townsend* in Section 5.1. The *scope* of the instructions will be significant for issues of privilege and disclosure: *Lucas v Barking, Havering and Redbridge NHS Trust* and other cases in Section 5.1.

Harmony Shipping Co v Saudi Europe Line Ltd (The Good Helm) (1979)

In a shipping dispute relating to a charterparty, the claimants sought the advice of a handwriting expert, but decided not to use him when he gave the opinion that the documents shown him were not genuine. The same expert was then consulted by the defendants. The claimants sought to prevent the expert from giving evidence for the defendants or assisting them in any way. The Court of Appeal upheld the judge's view that the defendants should be allowed to use the expert and rejected the argument that the expert was under a contractual duty to the claimants not to act against them.

> '... no such contract, express or implied, is to be found. At most there was a statement by [the expert witness] of his practice, namely, that, having been instructed by one side, he would not accept instructions from the other. That is a statement of a proper professional practice ... But it is not a contract ... If there was a contract by which a witness bound himself not to give evidence before the court on a matter on which the judge said he ought to give evidence ... any such contract would be contrary to public policy and would not be enforced by the court ... There is no property in an expert witness as to the facts he has observed and his own independent opinion on them. There being no such property in a witness, it is the duty of a witness to come to court and give his evidence insofar as he is directed by the judge to do so'.

Note that the remarks in the above case that it is undesirable for expert witnesses to be involved with both sides pre-date the Woolf recommendations on the use of SJEs and pre-date the CPR.

Yorke v Katra (2003)

The defendant client appealed against a striking out of his defence by a district judge in an action brought by the claimant contractor for payment. The defendant had accepted the appointment of a SJE to provide evidence on the quality of the work, but he objected to the joint instruction required by the judge and had asked why he could not provide a letter 'inviting the expert's report in this myself?'. The defence was struck out, but the Court of Appeal accepted the argument of the defendant's counsel based on CPR 35.7 and 35.8. CPR 35.8(1) provides that 'where the court gives a direction under rule 35.7 for a single joint expert to be used, each instructing party may give instructions to the expert'. The court also noted that in the notes to CPR 35.8 in the *White Book* (a practitioner's guide to civil court procedure), 'it is clearly envisaged that both parties may give instructions to an expert even though he is a joint expert'.

Allowing the appeal, the Court of Appeal rejected the district judge's approach:

'One can perhaps understand why the judge wanted there to be a single letter of instruction, but for my part it would not appear that she had jurisdiction to insist on that, as in fact she did, in view of the ability of each party to give separate instructions: and that manifestly is what Mr Katra wanted to do. He wanted the expert to have instructions from one side and from the other, and had produced instructions of his own, which was in fact in accordance with what was envisaged by the rules.'

6.2 THE REPORT AND THE EVIDENCE IT CONTAINS

The important part of an expert's report is the expert opinion which it contains, rather than a mere recital of the facts (although that may be unavoidable to some extent as well): *Ollett v Bristol Aerojet Ltd.* General guidance on how opinion evidence should be given is contained in *In Re J (A Minor)* (see Section 1 above). The report and its contents should be the product of the expert witness alone: *R v Balfour Beatty Civil Engineering* and *University of Warwick v Sir Robert McAlpine.*

If the report refers to research, articles, publications or other material, these will be admitted as part of the evidence and the expert can be cross-examined on them: *H v Schering Chemicals.* The CPR Part 35 Practice Direction sets out detailed requirements as to the form and content of the expert's report, including any literature or other material relied on. The Practice Direction lists other matters which must be contained in the report. Unless details of the qualifications of the expert witness are provided, the expert's appropriateness could not be ascertained: *Field v Leeds City Council* in Section 3.2. Development in the expert's thinking, or even changes of mind, need not be made explicit in the report, since any earlier drafts will be privileged: *Jackson v Marley Davenport Ltd*; although post-report changes must be communicated to the other side and to the court. However, any qualifications or reservations in the opinion must be stated under the Practice Direction and a declaration or statement of truth in the form supplied in para. 2.4 must also be given: *Phillips v Symes* in Section 3.1. Although reports are by CPR 35.11 available, once disclosed, to be used by any party as evidence at the trial, they do not become the property of the other party to be used in other proceedings: *Prudential Assurance v Fountain Page*. See also the new *Protocol on Amendment Reports*.

Ollett v Bristol Aerojet Ltd (1979)

In regretting an order by a registrar which did not require the substance of the respective experts' reports to be disclosed in a personal injury case, the judge made some observations on the ability of the expert witness to give opinion evidence:

> 'An expert, unlike other witnesses, is allowed, because of his special qualifications and/or experience, to give opinion evidence. It is for his opinion evidence that he is called, not for a factual description of the machine or the circumstances of the accident, although that is often necessary in order to explain and/or justify his conclusions. When the substance of the expert's report is to be provided, that means precisely what it says, both the substance of the factual description of the machine and/or the circumstances of the accident and his expert opinion in relation to that accident, which is the very justification for calling him.'

R v Balfour Beatty Civil Engineering Ltd (1999)

In prosecutions resulting from the 1994 Heathrow tunnel collapse under the *Health and Safety at Work Act* 1974, the judge (who had decided *The Ikarian Reefer*) commented on the shortcomings of the Health and Safety Executive's (HSE) expert evidence. The principal tunnelling expert, head of tunnelling at an engineering consultancy, had never before given expert evidence in a civil or criminal trial. After two days of the trial, the judge directed that the prosecution should identify those passages in the principal expert's report which emanated from the HSE. It transpired that 'extensive passages' in the report had been drafted by an HSE inspector; about 81 out of 122 pages of the main report contained contributions from HSE, 'sometimes extending to the whole of the page'. The whole of two appendices were drafted by the HSE inspector.

On the fourth day of the trial, the prosecution informed the court that it would no longer rely on the evidence of its principal expert. The court blamed the HSE for failing to give clear instructions to its staff 'as to the correct interface between a prosecuting authority and an expert witness' and the expert's failure 'to understand the duties and responsibilities of expert witnesses in criminal cases'. Although there was sufficient other evidence to secure a conviction, the judge made 'substantially reduced orders for costs against the defendants' to reflect the amount of trouble and expense caused to them by the flawed report.

University of Warwick v Sir Robert McAlpine (1988)

The observations of the judge on the role of expert witnesses were all obiter (i.e. not essential to the decision and therefore not strictly binding) in this case on negligent design and construction, but offer useful guidance on the role of experts, particularly in such cases.

The judge criticised the tendency of some of the experts to 'enter into the arena in order to advocate their client's case' leading to (justifiable) attacks by counsel on their credibility and veracity: 'This simply should not happen where the court is called upon to decide complex scientific or technical issues.'

The judge also objected to reports which 'contained the expertise of two or more experts'. If a non-signatory contributor to the report is not called, it places opposing counsel and the court in some difficulty as to how to scrutinise the evidence.

See on this latter point also *R v Balfour Beatty.*

H v Schering Chemicals Ltd (1983)

In an action concerning alleged injury caused by a drug manufactured by the defendant company, the judge considered the validity and value of a body of literature including research reports, articles and letters in medical journals and other documents. The defendants sought to have them excluded.

> 'These articles can be referred to by experts as part of the general corpus of medical knowledge falling within the expertise of an expert in this field. That of course means that an expert ... can fortify his opinion by referring to learned articles, publications, letters as reinforcing the view to which he has come. In doing so, he can make reference to papers in which a contrary opinion may be expressed but in which figures are set out which he regards as supporting his contention. In such a situation one asks: Are the figures and statistics set out in such an article strictly proved? and I think the answer is no. I think they are nonetheless of probative value when referred to and relied upon by an expert in the manner in which I have indicated. If an expert refers to the results of research published by a reputable authority in a reputable journal the court would, I think, ordinarily regard those results as supporting inferences fairly to be drawn from them, unless or until a different approach was shown to be proper.'

There will often be questions raised by the research and views contained in the material, which

> '... will fall to be considered and assessed when they are made and put to and discussed with any expert who relies on the articles. It may be that some of the answers will be found in the papers themselves. It may be that other matters will be left in doubt. It may very well be that

grounds will emerge for viewing the results of the research with caution or scepticism. But in my judgement the proper approach of the court is to admit the articles, in the sense of reading them, and to give the factual assertions in those articles such weight as appears to the court, having heard any cross-examination or other evidence, to be proper'.

Jackson v Marley Davenport Ltd (2004)

The claimant sued his defendant employer in a personal injury claim, following a fall from a ladder. For the purposes of a conference with the claimant's lawyers, the claimant's expert was instructed to prepare a report. When a report was subsequently served on the defendants by the claimant, the defendants concluded that the expert's opinion had changed and obtained an order for disclosure of the first report. However, this was reversed on appeal and the Court of Appeal upheld the claimant's position. The defendant argued that under CPR 35.13, the first report ought to be disclosed where an expert's view had 'developed' after fresh evidence. The Court of Appeal rejected this argument:

> 'There can be no doubt that, if an expert makes a report for the purpose of a party's legal advisors being able to give legal advice to their client, or for discussion in a conference of a party's legal advisers, such a report is the subject matter of litigation privilege at the time it is made. It has come into existence for the purposes of litigation. It is common for drafts of expert reports to be circulated among a party's advisers before a final report is prepared for exchange with the other side. Such initial reports are privileged.'

See *Carlton v Townsend*, which was applied in the above case.

Prudential Assurance Co Ltd v Fountain Page Ltd (1991)

Where an expert's report was exchanged before trial in an action which was then settled, the report could not be used in other related proceedings by the recipients, who were bringing an action in the Texas courts. The case concerned an action for breach of duty and deceit. The court held that disclosure of the expert's report to a third party would be a contempt of court and would be restrained.

6.3 EXAMINATION AND CROSS-EXAMINATION ON THE REPORT

Generally, a court or other tribunal will wish an expert witness to be examined, and especially cross-examined, as part of the process of appraisal of the evidence. Attempts to avoid cross-examination are therefore always likely to be treated with some scepticism. In *London & Leeds Estates Ltd v Paribas* (see Section 5.1), the expert was exposed to cross-examination on inconsistencies between his report on market conditions and evidence given in earlier separate arbitrations; the court would not protect him by holding them to be privileged.

However, the courts have developed some rules as to the limits on cross-examination: *Fairfield-Mabey Ltd v Shell UK Metallurgical Testing Services Ltd*. These have been especially necessary in the context of cross-examination of SJEs: *Austen v Oxford City Council* in Section 4.2.

Fairfield-Mabey Ltd v Shell UK Metallurgical Testing Services Ltd (1988)

The judge was asked during the trial to rule on manner of use of evidence of expert witnesses:

> '... it would be quite wrong for counsel in opening to refer to any witnesses' statement. It would also be wrong to cross examine a witness called by an opposing party by reference to a statement of another witness who might (or might not) be called in the future'.

An alternative is to put to the witness a statement taken on behalf of the cross-examiner's own client who thereby waives any confidentiality in the statement.

7

The tribunal's use of the expert witness's evidence

This section considers the weight given by courts and other tribunals to expert evidence, including the extent to which they are bound to accept it or are free to depart from it. The section is divided into three subsections:

7.1 The 'ultimate issue'
7.2 The effect of the expert evidence upon the tribunal's decision
7.3 The need for reasons

7.1 THE 'ULTIMATE ISSUE'

As was mentioned in Section 3.1, there is an important question as to what can be required of an expert witness, especially in professional negligence cases.

The traditional view has been that it is not permissible for experts to give their opinions on the law or on matters in issue, e.g. the negligence or otherwise of the defendant: *Crosfield (Joseph) and Sons Ltd v Techno-Chemical Laboratories Ltd* and *Midland Bank Trust Co Ltd v Hett Stubbs and Kemp* (see Section 3.1). However, a more pragmatic view has been taken in modern cases such as *Barings plc in Liquidation v Coopers & Lybrand* (Section 3.1) and *Routestone Ltd v Minories Finance Ltd*.

Crosfield (Joseph) and Sons Ltd v Techno-Chemical Laboratories Ltd (1913)

In a patent action concerning chemical compounds, the judge set out the purposes of calling expert witnesses in such cases, noting that there is no difference in regard to admissibility between patent cases and others.

> 'The assistance of expert evidence in patent actions is generally essential. It is required for the purpose of explaining words, or terms of science or art, appearing in the documents which have to be construed by the Court, or to inform the Court in case the import of a word or phrase differs from its popular meaning. Further than this, in some cases it is impossible for the Court to understand a document without instruction with regard to the laws of science with which the patent may be concerned without expert assistance. Moreover, the Court cannot inform itself as to the state of public knowledge with regard to the matters in question at the date of the patent.'

The court also expressed the view that it was not permissible for experts to give their opinions on the law or on matters in issue.

This last point is sometimes referred to in modern cases as the 'ultimate issue'. However, the latter approach has been modified in a number of subsequent cases: see *Barings v Coopers & Lybrand* and *Midland Bank v Hett Stubbs & Kemp*.

Routestone Ltd v Minories Finance Ltd (1997)

In a case in which negligence in marketing of a commercial property was alleged, the judge had to consider whether to accept the opinion of valuation experts on the 'ultimate question' of whether the defendants' estate agents had used reasonable care and skill (the agents were also sued).

Although the court paid careful regard to *Midland Bank v Hett Stubbs & Kemp*, it was held that the opinion of the valuer experts on negligence was admissible.

> 'What really matters in most cases is the reasons given for the opinion. As a practical matter a well constructed expert's report containing opinion evidence sets out the opinion and the reasons for it. If the reasons stand up, the opinion does, if not, not. A rule of evidence which excludes this opinion evidence serves no practical

purpose. What happens if the evidence is regarded as inadmissible is that the expert's reports simply try to creep up to the opinion without openly giving it. They insinuate rather than explicate.'

The distinction the judge drew was that in *Midland Bank v Hett Stubbs & Kemp* the court had objected to experts giving evidence as to the legal test, whereas here the expert's opinion was as to whether the defendants' conduct satisfied the legal test.

7.2 THE EFFECT OF THE EXPERT EVIDENCE UPON THE TRIBUNAL'S DECISION

The starting point must be that the court remains the ultimate decision-maker and that experts, however eminent, can do no more than provide evidence: *Davie v Magistrates of Edinburgh*. This is even true of a single joint expert (SJE), where the court is not compelled to accept the expert's evidence, even though none is forthcoming which contradicts it: *Coopers Payen Ltd v Southampton Container Terminal Ltd*. It is open to a court to prefer the evidence of 'honest lay claimants' (for example) to that of expert witnesses: *Armstrong v First York Ltd*. In extreme cases, even the existence of a body of professional opinion might not be decisive if the judge was satisfied that that opinion was unreasonable: *Bolitho v City and Hackney Health Authority*, *Calver v Westwood Veterinary Group* and *Kapadia v London Borough of Lambeth*. The tribunal should not simply adopt the view of the expert witness instead of making its own critical assessment: *Abadeh v British Telecommunications Ltd*, *Patel v Mehtab* and *O'Toole v Knowsley Metropolitan Borough Council* (see Section 3.2).

However, there is a balance to be struck between the tribunal retaining the power to decide and the substitution of an unqualified lay opinion for an expert one: *Dover District Council v Sherred*.

Where there is an agreed experts' report on the facts, the judge will normally be wrong to seek to go behind the report and to undo the findings: *Stringfellow v Blyth*.

There are two main keys to understanding the balance between the tribunal's ultimate responsibility to make the decision, while not simply substituting an inexpert opinion for an expert one. First, the tribunal must consider all the evidence together: *EPI Environmental Technologies Inc and another v Symphony Plastic Technologies plc and another* and *Youssif v Jordan*. Second, which forms the last part of this section, the tribunal may have an obligation to give reasons if departing from the evidence of experts.

Certain types of case will normally require expert evidence, most notably professional negligence claims: *Worboys v Acme Investments* in Section 3.1; although even here it is open to a court to find such evidence not to be 'a necessary precondition': *Merivale Moore plc v Strutt & Parker*. Conversely, appellate courts will, by definition, always suffer from the absence of first-hand experience of the giving of the expert evidence, so that only exceptionally should they disturb findings based on it: *Maynard v West Midlands Regional Health Authority*.

Davie v Magistrates of Edinburgh (1953)

In an action by a neighbouring owner respecting damage caused to his property by blasting operations during sewer construction, issues arose as to the weight to be given to the evidence of expert witnesses called, including a builder, an architect and a civil engineer.

The judges made some observations on the weight and value to be given to the opinions of expert scientific witnesses.

'I do not consider that in the case of expert opinion evidence formal corroboration is required in the same way as it is required for proof of an essential fact, however desirable it may be in some cases to be able to rely upon two or more experts rather than upon one. The value of such evidence depends upon the authority, experience and qualifications of the expert and above all upon the extent to which his evidence carries conviction, and not upon the possibility of producing a second person to echo the sentiments of the first ...'

The defenders had gone so far, however, as to argue that the court was bound to accept the evidence of one of their experts:

'This view I must firmly reject as contrary to the principles in accordance with which expert opinion evidence is admitted. Expert witnesses, however skilled or eminent, can give no more than evidence. They cannot usurp the functions of the jury or the Judge sitting as a jury, any more than a technical assessor can substitute his advice for the judgment of the Court ... Their duty is to furnish the Judge or jury with the necessary scientific criteria for testing the accuracy of their conclusions, so as to enable the Judge or jury to form their own independent judgment by the application of these criteria to the facts proved in evidence. The scientific opinion evidence, if intelligible, convincing and tested, becomes a factor (and often an important factor) for consideration along with the whole other evidence in the case, but the decision is for the Judge or jury.'

Coopers Payen Ltd v Southampton Container Terminal Ltd (2003)

In an action for damages to a press which fell from a trailer at Southampton Container Terminal, the Court of Appeal considered the extent to which a judge would be entitled to depart from the evidence of a single expert.

The court accepted the authority of Lord Woolf's principles in *Peet v Mid-Kent Health Care Trust* but also counsel's submission that the case 'does not establish that the evidence of the expert must then be accepted by the court. The court must take its own view of the expert evidence in the light of all the other evidence'.

The Court of Appeal's view was that:

'All depends upon the circumstances of the particular case. For example, the joint expert may be the only witness on a particular topic, as for instance where the facts on which he expresses an opinion are agreed. In such circumstances it is difficult to envisage a case in which it would be appropriate to decide this case on the basis that the expert's opinion was wrong. More often, however, the expert's opinion will only be part of the evidence in the case ... at the end of the trial the duty of the court is to apply the burden of proof and to find the facts having regard to all the evidence in the case, which will or may include both evidence of fact and evidence of opinion which may interrelate.'

Further:

'Where a single expert gives evidence on an issue of fact on which no direct evidence is called, for example as to valuation, then subject to the need to evaluate his evidence in the light of his answers in cross-examination his evidence is likely to prove compelling. Only in exceptional circumstances may the judge depart from it and then for a good reason which he must fully explain.'

However, where an expert's evidence is on an issue of fact where it is challenged by direct evidence to the contrary, such as on the speed of a vehicle,

'There is no rule of law or practice in such a situation requiring the judge to favour or accept the evidence of the expert or the evidence of a witness of fact. The judge must consider whether he can reconcile the evidence of the expert witness with that of the witness of fact. If he cannot do so, he must consider whether there may be an explanation for the conflict of evidence or for a possible error by either witness, and in the light of all the circumstances make a considered choice which evidence to accept.'

Armstrong v First York Ltd (2005)

There is no rule of law preventing a judge from preferring the evidence of honest lay claimants (in a personal injury claim in this case) to that of a jointly instructed expert, even though the judge was unable to explain why he found fault with the expert's evidence. The defendants' submission that the judge had no choice but to accept the expert's evidence if he was unable to point to an error in it was incorrect:

'In this jurisdiction, reliance is placed upon trial by judge, and not by expert, and the judge is fully entitled to weigh all the evidence, as he has done.'

Bolitho v City and Hackney Health Authority (1998)

In this medical negligence case, the House of Lords considered how expert evidence as to a body of professional opinion in a professional negligence case should be dealt with.

> '… in cases of diagnosis and treatment there are cases where, despite a body of professional opinion sanctioning the defendant's conduct, the defendant can properly be held liable for negligence … that is because, in some cases, it cannot be demonstrated to the judge's satisfaction that the body of opinion relied upon is reasonable or responsible. In the vast majority of cases the fact that distinguished experts in the field are of a particular opinion will demonstrate the reasonableness of that opinion … But if, in a rare case, it can be demonstrated that the professional opinion is not capable of withstanding logical analysis, the judge is entitled to hold that the body of opinion is not reasonable or responsible.
>
> I emphasise that in my view it will very seldom be right for a judge to reach the conclusion that views generally held by a competent medical expert are unreasonable. The assessment of medical risks and benefits is a matter of clinical judgment which a judge would not normally be able to make without expert evidence … It is only where a judge can be satisfied that the body of expert opinion cannot be logically supported at all that such opinion will not provide the benchmark by reference to which the defendant's conduct falls to be assessed'.

See *Calver v Westwood Veterinary Group,* where the above principles were followed.

Calver v Westwood Veterinary Group (2001)

In a case brought against a veterinary surgeon for alleged negligent treatment of a pregnant mare, the court gave indications as to how expert evidence as to a body of professional opinion should be treated. The court applied the principles set out in *Bolitho v City and Hackney Health Authority*.

Kapadia v London Borough of Lambeth (2000)

An employee of the council who had taken substantial amounts of time off work with depression was retired on medical grounds. He claimed disability discrimination and two experts gave evidence of an underlying disability. No evidence from the local authority was called to challenge this, but the employment tribunal rejected the discrimination claim. The Employment Appeal Tribunal (EAT) allowed the employee's appeal and this was upheld by the Court of Appeal.

> 'The direct evidence ... came from two medical experts ... There was no contrary expert medical evidence. There was no challenge to the factual bases of those opinions. Nor were there any peculiar circumstances which would enable those opinions to be challenged ... [T]he employment tribunal was obliged to come to the conclusion that the employee had proved his case and erred in not so doing.'

Further:

> 'There will be cases in which a fact-finding tribunal is not obliged to accept uncontested medical evidence given to it. For example, the evidence on the basis of which a doctor has formed an opinion may be rejected by the fact-finding tribunal. There may be cases where it is clear that the medical witness has misunderstood the evidence which he was invited to consider in expressing his opinion. No such considerations apply, however, in this case.'

Note that, in a separate finding, the Court of Appeal held that the employee's agreement to be examined by the council's experts constituted implied consent for the experts' reports to be shown to the council; no further permission was needed.

Dover District Council v Sherred (1997)

In an appeal by the council against a notice of repair of its housing under the *Housing Act* 1985, the council argued that the judge had substituted his own opinion for that of the expert witnesses on the question of fitness for human habitation. The court, dismissing the appeal, set out the relationship between the expert evidence and the judge's decision, approving *Patel v Mehtab*.

The court

'… would prefer to stick to the general rule that issues of fact are for the judge to decide in accordance with the evidence given before him. Where expert evidence is admissible in order to enable the judge to reach a properly informed decision on a technical matter, then he cannot set his own "lay" opinion against the expert evidence that he has heard. But he is not bound to accept the evidence even of an expert witness, if there is a proper basis for rejecting it in the other evidence that he has heard, or the expert evidence is such that he does not believe it or for whatever reason is not convinced by it'.

Abadeh v British Telecommunications plc (2001)

The EAT held that the employment tribunal had been wrong in its evaluation of the medical evidence; it had been over-influenced by the evidence of the employers' regional medical officer as to whether the applicant's impairments were 'substantial' for the purposes of the *Disability Discrimination Act* 1995. The effect was that the tribunal had simply adopted the view of the expert witness instead of making their own assessment.

Patel v Mehtab (1980)

Magistrates concluded that there was no statutory nuisance in premises 'in such a state as to be prejudicial to health' under the then *Public Health Act* 1936, even though an environmental health officer and a public health consultant had given evidence that the premises were injurious to health.

The court allowed the appeal against this finding:

'In deciding some questions of fact, magistrates are entitled to draw on their own personal experience, either of the locality or of life in general. But when it comes to deciding whether the condition of premises is or is not liable or likely to be injurious to health, one is moving outside the field where a tribunal is entitled to draw on its own experience. That is a matter upon which the tribunal needs informed expert evidence. This tribunal had informed expert evidence and, bearing in mind that they were not entitled to substitute their own opinion, the evidence was all one way … it is a case in which the magistrates have misdirected themselves.'

Stringfellow v Blyth (2001)

In a dispute in the Technology and Construction Court concerning building work at a house, the two experts instructed respectively by the claimant and the defendant reported on the dimensions of the walls. The claimant's expert maintained that they had agreed a conclusion on this point, although the defendant's expert denied this. In an interlocutory application, another judge found that there was agreement, but the trial judge disregarded the agreed experts' report and allowed the defendant to give oral evidence on the walls point. The Court of Appeal held that the trial judge ought not to have gone behind what had been held to be an agreed experts' report and the appeal was therefore allowed.

EPI Environmental Technologies Inc and another v Symphony Plastic Technologies plc and another (2005)

It is essential for judges to evaluate the evidence of witnesses (expert and non-expert) in its entirety. Errors, or even lies, in evidence would not automatically deprive the rest of the evidence of the witness of its value.

It is also essential that witnesses are challenged with the other side's case. Failure to put a point forward should usually disentitle the point from being taken in a closing address.

A judge is rarely helped by competing experts' reports which express opinions not tested or not maintainable by reference to supporting material. It is not useful simply to leave the judge to find his own analysis of experts' reports without them being put to the test of cross-examination.

Youssif v Jordan (2004)

In a medical negligence case, the judge was held on appeal to have been wrong to make a finding of no case to answer. The judge had failed to appreciate the conflict of evidence between expert witnesses who were not called to give oral evidence. There is a danger inherent in defendants doing well in litigation and proceeding to a submission of no case to answer. In such circumstances, it is the judge's duty to survey the evidence of the expert witnesses as a whole together with that of the defendant, to see whether the claimant might make out his case.

Merivale Moore plc v Strutt & Parker (1999)

The defendant valuers sought to argue that, before their valuation of property could be condemned as outside the range that could be reached by any competent valuer, and therefore negligent, the claimants would have to produce expert evidence to that effect. Although the court agreed that, with such evidence, the judge's task is 'substantially eased', it would not accept

> '... that the adduction of such evidence is a necessary precondition to the finding of negligence on the part of a valuer ... it is still open to the judge in a suitable case to hold that the valuation is so far removed from what was the true value of the property that it must be regarded as a valuation that was outside the limits open to a competent valuer, without specific professional evidence being given of what those limits were'.

Maynard v West Midlands Regional Health Authority (1985)

In a medical negligence case, the House of Lords considered the role of an appellate court in reviewing the conclusions of the trial judge on the evidence of expert witnesses. They approved the approach taken in *Whitehouse v Jordan* to the effect that the advantages of the trial judge in seeking and hearing the witnesses must always at least be respected. The advantages of a trial judge were also considered by the Court of Appeal.

The House of Lords stated that the relevant principles remain that

> '... an appellate court, if disposed to come to a different conclusion from the trial judge on the printed evidence, should not do so unless satisfied that the advantage enjoyed by him of seeing and hearing the witnesses is not sufficient to explain or justify his conclusion. But if the appellate court is satisfied that he has not made a proper use of his advantage, "the matter will then become at large for the appellate court" '.

In this case, the Court of Appeal and the House of Lords were satisfied that the judge had not fully understood the expert evidence in reaching his conclusions on the negligence allegations.

7.3 THE NEED FOR REASONS

As a matter of general principle and practice, judges give some explanation for their decisions, although they are not obliged to justify every finding. To a limited extent, a judge may not have to say exactly why he/she finds fault with expert evidence: *Armstrong v First York* in Section 7.2. However, expert evidence is usually treated somewhat differently and it is fair to say that a greater effort is to be expected from a tribunal to explain why it does not accept such evidence in reaching its decision: *Eckersley v Binnie* and *Flannery v Halifax Estate Agencies*. The Court of Appeal has emphasised that this would be especially true in the case of a professional negligence claim: *Cheal v Hale Allen*. In the SJE case of *Stephens v Cannon*, the judge, unable to decide which expert to prefer, simply fell back on the burden of proof, but the Court of Appeal criticised the judge's failure to work through the issues between the experts, finding his way to a conclusion without resort to the burden of proof.

Eckersley v Binnie (1988)

Following the death of 16 visitors to a pumping station due to a methane explosion (the Abbeystead disaster), negligence actions were brought by survivors and relatives of the deceased against those responsible for the design, construction and operation of the works. The first instance judge having given findings on the extensive expert evidence presented by all sides, the Court of Appeal ruled on its own review function in relation to those findings:

> 'In resolving conflicts of expert evidence, the judge remains the judge; he is not obliged to accept evidence simply because it comes from an illustrious source; he can take account of demonstrated partisanship and lack of objectivity. But save where an expert is guilty of a deliberate attempt to mislead (as happens only very rarely), a coherent reasoned opinion expressed by a suitably qualified expert should be the subject of a coherent reasoned rebuttal, unless it can be discounted for other good reason.'

Flannery v Halifax Estate Agencies Ltd (1999)

The first instance judge in this negligent valuation case had given judgment for the defendant valuers against the claimant mortgagors with the simple statement that he preferred the evidence of the defendants' experts. The Court of Appeal held that the failure of a trial judge to give reasons for conclusions reached at first instance could of itself constitute a good ground of appeal. This is especially so in cases involving expert evidence.

> 'That today's professional judge owes a general duty to give reasons is clear ... although there are some exceptions ... It is not a useful task to attempt to make absolute rules as to the requirement for the judge to give reasons ... For instance, when the court, in a case without documents, depending on eye-witness accounts, is faced with two irreconcilable accounts, there may be little to say other than that the witnesses for one side were more credible ... But with expert evidence, it should usually be possible to be more explicit in giving reasons ...'

See *Eckersley v Binnie*, which the court applied.

Cheal v Hale Allen (1997)

In making a finding of professional negligence against a defendant, a court would have to give explicit reasons for not accepting evidence of an expert witness in the defendant's favour. The Court of Appeal allowed an appeal from a finding of negligence against a defendant chartered structural engineer who had advised the claimant on the purchase of a house. The judge had preferred the evidence of the claimant's expert.

> 'When a man's professional reputation is at stake the court will normally find it necessary to explain with some care precisely why he was at fault especially if, as here, the defendant is supported by an independent expert, with appropriate experience and standing who says in effect that even with the benefit of hindsight he would have reported just as the defendant did.

> In this case the judge simply summarised the evidence of [the defendant's expert, the defendant and the claimant's expert] ... he said: "I prefer the evidence of [the claimant's expert] to that of [the defendant and his expert]." ... That I find to be contrary to a formidable body of evidence which I have attempted to summarise and which the judgment of the judge simply does not address.'

Further:

> 'The judge did not explain why he found the evidence of the defendant and in particular the evidence of his expert witness ... to be unacceptable. As I have already indicated, it is my view that if their evidence was to be rejected such an explanation was required.'

Stephens v Cannon (2005)

Following the appointment of a SJE in a property development dispute, one of the parties got permission to instruct their own expert witness. The SJE valued at £1.9m and the party-appointed expert at £1.5m, a building which existed only in the form of plans. The master hearing the case stated that he found it impossible to prefer one to the other, since he would be setting himself up as an expert and usurping the experts' role. He therefore fell back on the burden of proof; since neither expert's evidence was preferred, the claimants had failed to discharge the burden of proof and the defendants' view must succeed.

The Court of Appeal, allowing the appeal, criticised the master's approach:

'... had he sought to work his way through the specific issues between the experts as to the effect on value of the allegedly positive and negative features of [the subject property], he might well, in the light also of the other evidence, have found his way to a conclusion, one way or another, without resort to the burden of proof'.

The court set out a series of propositions as to when a tribunal could rely on the burden of proof:

(1) The situation in which the court finds itself before it can despatch a disputed issue by resort to the burden of proof has to be exceptional.
(2) The issue does not have to be of any particular type; a legitimate 'state of agnosticism' can arise following enquiry into any type of disputed issue.
(3) The exceptional situation which entitles the court to resort to the burden of proof is that, notwithstanding that it has striven to do so, it cannot reasonably make a finding in relation to a disputed issue.
(4) A court which resorts to the burden of proof must ensure that others can discern that it has striven to make a finding in relation to a disputed issue and can understand the reasons why it has concluded that it cannot do so.
(5) In a few cases the fact of the endeavour and the reasons for the conclusion will be self-evident, however, in most cases, the judgment must contain explanation and reasons.

8
Post-hearing matters

It is convenient in this final section to deal with two otherwise unrelated matters which will normally only arise at the conclusion of the hearing. These are:

8.1 The costs of the expert witness
8.2 Expert witness immunity

8.1 THE COSTS OF THE EXPERT WITNESS

Under CPR 35.4(4), the court has power to limit the amount of the expert's recoverable fees and expenses: such a limit was imposed on a SJE in *Kranidiotes v Paschali* (see Section 4.2). What is and what is not recoverable is likely to be of considerable importance to the parties in any event, and the courts have been called upon to make decisions and establish rules on a number of occasions. In *Brown v Bennett* (see Section 4.1), it was a party's inability to continue to pay the expert's fees which forced them to seek an order compelling his attendance.

Normally, professional expert witnesses will charge according to their usual fee scales or structures, although fees can still be claimed whether or not the expert belongs to a professional body: *Longley v South West Regional Health Authority* (in Section 3.2). Two particularly contentious areas are (a) the extent to which parties can claim the costs of their own staff acting as 'in-house' experts and (b) the point at which the expert's costs begin to run, which may in reality be well before the issue of proceedings: *In Re Nossen's Letters Patent* and *Admiral Management Services Ltd v Para-Protect Ltd.*

Note that the court can make a costs order against the expert him/herself in appropriate circumstances: *Phillips v Symes* (see Section 3.1).

In Re Nossen's Letter Patent (1969)

In a patent dispute, the court had to consider the extent to which costs should be allowed for work by the employees of one of the parties in providing expert advice and services in preparation of the claim.

> 'The established practice of the courts has been to disallow any sums claimed in respect of the time spent by the litigant personally in the course of instructing his solicitors. In the case of litigation by a corporation, this has not been strictly applied, for it has been recognised that, if expert assistance is properly required, it may well occur that the corporation's own specialist employees may be the most suitable or convenient experts to employ. If the corporation litigant does decide to provide expert assistance from its own staff ... the taxing master has to determine the appropriate charge to allow. For the outside expert, the normal assessment would be based on current professional standards, and this in suitable cases would include a proper proportion of the overhead costs of running his office or laboratory, that is, of the costs necessarily incurred by him in his capacity as a consultant, as well as a profit element upon such expenditure ... No part of the respondents' expenditure on overheads was occasioned by this litigation and it would be unreasonable to transfer to the applicant the burden of meeting some part of it by reason only of the respondents' decision to prefer the services of their own staff to those of independent experts ... when it is appropriate that a corporate litigant should recover, on a party and party basis, a sum in respect of expert services of this character performed by its own staff, the amount must be restricted to a reasonable sum for the actual and direct costs of the work undertaken.'

Admiral Management Services Ltd v Para-Protect Ltd (2002)

In some circumstances, it will be possible to claim as the costs of litigation (or, by analogy, arbitration) fees and other expenses incurred by experts before commencement of the action by the issue of proceedings. This may even sometimes extend to work done by a party's own in-house experts, provided the evidence being prepared (for example, to evaluate the chances of bringing a successful claim) is genuinely that of an expert, and not merely gathering of facts and provided it avoids the necessity of employing an external expert. Although, in general, work by a litigant's employee in investigating and preparing material for legal proceedings would not be claimable as costs in the action, the above could, in appropriate circumstances, constitute an exception.

This case concerned alleged improper use by the defendants of confidential information belonging to the claimants. Note that the experts involved in preparing the claim may or may not be used subsequently as expert witnesses. The judge noted that there are now 'special rules applicable to expert witnesses, leading to a distinction between an expert adviser and an expert witness instructed to prepare a report for the court'.

8.2 EXPERT WITNESS IMMUNITY

The basic position is that an expert witness is immune from suit in respect of his/her report and the evidence given at trial, as set out in the Court of Appeal's leading decision of *Stanton v Callaghan*. It is confirmed in that case, and previously in *Palmer v Durnford Ford*, that this immunity does *not* extend to preliminary work. The justification for immunity was considered by the House of Lords in *Saif Ali v Sydney Mitchell & Co*. The most recent consideration of the issue can be found in the Scots case of *Karling v Purdue*.

Stanton and Stanton v Callaghan (1999)

The following propositions were stated to be binding in law, in a case where the claimants tried to sue their expert witness for changing his position in reaching agreement with the defendants' expert. They represent an important contribution to the modern position on the immunity of an expert witness:

(1) An expert witness who gives evidence at a trial is immune from suit in respect of anything which he says

in court, and that immunity will extend to the contents of the report which he adopts as, or incorporates in his evidence.

(2) Where an expert witness gives evidence at a trial, the immunity which he would enjoy in respect of that evidence is not to be circumvented by a suit based on the report itself.

(3) The immunity does not extend to protect an expert who has been retained to advise as to the merits of a party's claim in litigation from a suit by the party by whom he has been retained in respect of that advice.

The Court of Appeal allowed the appeal of the defendant expert and struck out the claim against him.

Palmer v Durnford Ford (1992)

In a case concerning damages for repair of a lorry tractor unit which had broken down, the claimants had to abandon their claim as hopeless and sued their experts, whom it was alleged lacked the necessary qualifications to advise and should not have accepted the retainer. The experts, pleading immunity, sought to have the claim struck out. However, the judge distinguished between giving evidence in court and preliminary work:

'I can see no good reason why an expert should not be liable for the advice which he gives to his client as to the merits of the claim, particularly if proceedings have not been started, and *a fortiori* [i.e. even more so] as to whether he is qualified to advise at all ... The problem is where to draw the line given that there is immunity for evidence given in court and it must extend to the preparation of such evidence to avoid the immunity being outflanked and rendered of little use ... The immunity would only extend to what could fairly be said to be preliminary to his giving evidence in the court, judged perhaps by the principal purpose for which the work was done. So the production or approval of a report for the purposes of disclosure to the other side would be immune but work done for the principal purpose of advising the client would not ... I do not think that difficulty in drawing the line precisely should result in a [claimant] in a case such as this being denied all remedy against his expert.'

See also *Stanton v Callaghan* in which the above case was approved.

Saif Ali v Sydney Mitchell & Co (1980)

In a case concerning the issue of a barrister's immunity from a civil action for negligence in representing a client in litigation, the House of Lords considered the 'general immunity from civil liability which attaches to all persons in respect of their participation in proceedings before a court of justice'. This immunity includes witnesses and is based on public policy 'to ensure that trials are conducted without avoidable stress and tensions of alarm and fear in those who have a part to play in them'.

Lord Diplock quoted *Cabassi v Vila* in the High Court of Australia: 'The law protects witnesses and others, not for their benefit, but for a higher interest, namely, the advancement of public justice'; and *Watson v McEwan* to the effect that 'the immunity of witnesses extends not only to the evidence they give in court but to statements made by the witness to the client and to the solicitor in preparing the witness's proof for the trial since, unless these statements were protected, the protection to which the witness would be entitled at the trial could be circumvented'.

Note that confusion is sometimes caused by cases such as *Zubaida v Hargreaves*, where an expert engaged by the parties to determine a rent review was sued for negligence. This does not affect the immunity of an expert *witness* in respect of litigation. The confusion arises merely from the practice of referring to expert witnesses as 'experts' for the sake of brevity.

Karling v Purdue (2004)

In an action by a previously accused person in criminal proceedings against a pathologist responsible for flawed Crown evidence, the court considered the scope of an expert's immunity from suit. The following principles would apply generally:

(1) When a witness comes to court to give evidence, he is immune from any civil action that might be brought against him on the ground that the things said or done by him in the ordinary course of proceedings were said or done negligently.

(2) The underlying rationale of the immunity is that witnesses should speak freely. Without the rule, witnesses would be reluctant to assist the court.

(3) The immunity would be worthless if confined to the actual giving of evidence in court. The immunity applies to potential or prospective witnesses who might not, in the event, be called to give evidence.

(4) Moreover, immunity applies to the early stages of litigation where evidence is being collected with a view to court proceedings.

(5) Negligent conduct, such as examination or removal of organs in a post-mortem examination, for the purposes of making a report with a view to giving evidence will be protected on the ground that the conduct forms part of the preparation by a potential witness.

(6) Absolute immunity exists where the statement or conduct is such that it can fairly be said to be part of the process of investigating a crime or possible crime with a view to a prosecution or a possible prosecution in respect of the matter being investigated.

(7) Where investigations have an immediate link with possible proceedings, immunity applies.

(8) Where an expert is engaged in the context of an existing litigation or a prospective litigation, he may perform a dual role. The first is advisory and the second is in his capacity as expert witness. The difficulty of identifying whether the work of an expert or part of it falls within or outwith the protective circle of immunity is greater in the context of civil proceedings than criminal proceedings.

(9) The acts of an expert which are intimately connected with the conduct of the litigation and those which are not is a distinction which is very difficult to apply with any degree of consistency and may not truly represent the touchstone of immunity.

Appendix 1
CPR 35 – Experts and Assessors

Crown copyright material is reproduced with the permission of the Controller of HMSO and the Queen's Printer for Scotland.

Contents of this Part

Duty to restrict expert evidence

35.1 Expert evidence shall be restricted to that which is reasonably required to resolve the proceedings.

Interpretation

35.2 A reference to an 'expert' in this Part is a reference to an expert who has been instructed to give or prepare evidence for the purpose of court proceedings.

Experts – overriding duty to the court

35.3 (1) It is the duty of an expert to help the court on the matters within his expertise.

(2) This duty overrides any obligation to the person from whom he has received instructions or by whom he is paid.

Court's power to restrict expert evidence

35.4 (1) No party may call an expert or put in evidence an expert's report without the court's permission.

(2) When a party applies for permission under this rule he must identify –

(a) the field in which he wishes to rely on expert evidence; and

(b) where practicable the expert in that field on whose evidence he wishes to rely.

(3) If permission is granted under this rule it shall be in relation only to the expert named or the field identified under paragraph (2).

(4) The court may limit the amount of the expert's fees and expenses that the party who wishes to rely on the expert may recover from any other party.

General requirement for expert evidence to be given in a written report

35.5 (1) Expert evidence is to be given in a written report unless the court directs otherwise.

(2) If a claim is on the fast track, the court will not direct an expert to attend a hearing unless it is necessary to do so in the interests of justice.

Written questions to experts

35.6 (1) A party may put to –

(a) an expert instructed by another party; or

(b) a single joint expert appointed under rule 35.7, written questions about his report.

(2) Written questions under paragraph (1) –
  (a) may be put once only;
  (b) must be put within 28 days of service of the expert's report; and
  (c) must be for the purpose only of clarification of the report,
  unless in any case,
    (i) the court gives permission; or
    (ii) the other party agrees.

(3) An expert's answers to questions put in accordance with paragraph (1) shall be treated as part of the expert's report.

(4) Where –
  (a) a party has put a written question to an expert instructed by another party in accordance with this rule; and
  (b) the expert does not answer that question,
  the court may make one or both of the following orders in relation to the party who instructed the expert –
    (i) that the party may not rely on the evidence of that expert; or
    (ii) that the party may not recover the fees and expenses of that expert from any other party.

Court's power to direct that evidence is to be given by a single joint expert

35.7 (1) Where two or more parties wish to submit expert evidence on a particular issue, the court may direct that the evidence on that issue is to given by one expert only.

(2) The parties wishing to submit the expert evidence are called 'the instructing parties'.

(3) Where the instructing parties cannot agree who should be the expert, the court may –
  (a) select the expert from a list prepared or identified by the instructing parties; or
  (b) direct that the expert be selected in such other manner as the court may direct.

Instructions to a single joint expert

35.8 (1) Where the court gives a direction under rule 35.7 for a single joint expert to be used, each instructing party may give instructions to the expert.

(2) When an instructing party gives instructions to the expert he must, at the same time, send a copy of the instructions to the other instructing parties.

(3) The court may give directions about –
   (a) the payment of the expert's fees and expenses; and
   (b) any inspection, examination or experiments which the expert wishes to carry out.

(4) The court may, before an expert is instructed –
   (a) limit the amount that can be paid by way of fees and expenses to the expert; and
   (b) direct that the instructing parties pay that amount into court.

(5) Unless the court otherwise directs, the instructing parties are jointly and severally liable for the payment of the expert's fees and expenses.

Power of court to direct a party to provide information

35.9 Where a party has access to information which is not reasonably available to the other party, the court may direct the party who has access to the information to –
   (a) prepare and file a document recording the information; and
   (b) serve a copy of that document on the other party.

Contents of report

35.10 (1) An expert's report must comply with the requirements set out in the relevant practice direction.

(2) At the end of an expert's report there must be a statement that –
   (a) the expert understands his duty to the court; and
   (b) he has complied with that duty.

(3) The expert's report must state the substance of all material instructions, whether written or oral, on the basis of which the report was written.

(4) The instructions referred to in paragraph (3) shall not be privileged against disclosure but the court will not, in relation to those instructions –
   (a) order disclosure of any specific document; or
   (b) permit any questioning in court, other than by the party who instructed the expert,
   unless it is satisfied that there are reasonable grounds to consider the statement of instructions given under paragraph (3) to be inaccurate or incomplete.

Use by one party of expert's report disclosed by another

35.11 Where a party has disclosed an expert's report, any party may use that expert's report as evidence at the trial.

Discussions between experts

35.12 (1) The court may, at any stage, direct a discussion between experts for the purpose of requiring the experts to –
   (a) identify and discuss the expert issues in the proceedings; and
   (b) where possible, reach an agreed opinion on those issues.
(2) The court may specify the issues which the experts must discuss.
(3) The court may direct that following a discussion between the experts they must prepare a statement for the court showing –
   (a) those issues on which they agree; and
   (b) those issues on which they disagree and a summary of their reasons for disagreeing.
(4) The content of the discussion between the experts shall not be referred to at the trial unless the parties agree.
(5) Where experts reach agreement on an issue during their discussions, the agreement shall not bind the parties unless the parties expressly agree to be bound by the agreement.

Consequence of failure to disclose expert's report

35.13 A party who fails to disclose an expert's report may not use the report at the trial or call the expert to give evidence orally unless the court gives permission.

Expert's right to ask court for directions

35.14 (1) An expert may file a written request for directions to assist him in carrying out his function as an expert.

(2) An expert must, unless the court orders otherwise, provide a copy of any proposed request for directions under paragraph (1)–

(a) to the party instructing him, at least 7 days before he files the request; and

(b) to all other parties, at least 4 days before he files it.

(3) The court, when it gives directions, may also direct that a party be served with a copy of the directions.

Assessors

35.15 (1) This rule applies where the court appoints one or more persons (an 'assessor') under section 70 of the Supreme Court Act 1981 or section 63 of the County Courts Act 1984.

(2) The assessor shall assist the court in dealing with a matter in which the assessor has skill and experience.

(3) An assessor shall take such part in the proceedings as the court may direct and in particular the court may –

(a) direct the assessor to prepare a report for the court on any matter at issue in the proceedings; and

(b) direct the assessor to attend the whole or any part of the trial to advise the court on any such matter.

(4) If the assessor prepares a report for the court before the trial has begun –

(a) the court will send a copy to each of the parties; and

(b) the parties may use it at trial.

(5) The remuneration to be paid to the assessor for his services shall be determined by the court and shall form part of the costs of the proceedings.

(6) The court may order any party to deposit in the court office a specified sum in respect of the assessor's fees and, where it does so, the assessor will not be asked to act until the sum has been deposited.

(7) Paragraphs (5) and (6) do not apply where the remuneration of the assessor is to be paid out of money provided by Parliament.

Appendix 2
CPR 35 Practice Direction – Experts and Assessors

Crown copyright material is reproduced with the permission of the Controller of HMSO and the Queen's Printer for Scotland.

THIS PRACTICE DIRECTION SUPPLEMENTS
CPR PART 35

Part 35 is intended to limit the use of oral expert evidence to that which is reasonably required. In addition, where possible, matters requiring expert evidence should be dealt with by a single expert. Permission of the court is always required either to call an expert or to put an expert's report in evidence.

Expert Evidence – General Requirements

1.1 It is the duty of an expert to help the court on matters within his own expertise: rule 35.3(1). This duty is paramount and overrides any obligation to the person from whom the expert has received instructions or by whom he is paid: rule 35.3(2).

1.2 Expert evidence should be the independent product of the expert uninfluenced by the pressures of litigation.

1.3 An expert should assist the court by providing objective, unbiased opinion on matters within his expertise, and should not assume the role of an advocate.

1.4 An expert should consider all material facts, including those which might detract from his opinion.

1.5 An expert should make it clear:
 (a) when a question or issue falls outside his expertise; and
 (b) when he is not able to reach a definite opinion, for example because he has insufficient information.

1.6 If, after producing a report, an expert changes his view on any material matter, such change of view should be communicated to all the parties without delay, and when appropriate to the court.

Form and Content of Expert's Reports

2.1 An expert's report should be addressed to the court and not to the party from whom the expert has received his instructions.

2.2 An expert's report must:

(1) give details of the expert's qualifications;

(2) give details of any literature or other material which the expert has relied on in making the report;

(3) contain a statement setting out the substance of all facts and instructions given to the expert which are material to the opinions expressed in the report or upon which those opinions are based;

(4) make clear which of the facts stated in the report are within the expert's own knowledge;

(5) say who carried out any examination, measurement, test or experiment which the expert has used for the report, give the qualifications of that person, and say whether or not the test or experiment has been carried out under the expert's supervision;

(6) where there is a range of opinion on the matters dealt with in the report –

(a) summarise the range of opinion, and

(b) give reasons for his own opinion;

(7) contain a summary of the conclusions reached;

(8) if the expert is not able to give his opinion without qualification, state the qualification; and

(9) contain a statement that the expert understands his duty to the court, and has complied and will continue to comply with that duty.

2.3 An expert's report must be verified by a statement of truth as well as containing the statements required in paragraph 2.2(8) and (9) above.

2.4 The form of the statement of truth is as follows:

'I confirm that insofar as the facts stated in my report are within my own knowledge I have made clear which they are and I believe them to be true, and that the opinions I have expressed represent my true and complete professional opinion.'

2.5 Attention is drawn to rule 32.14 which sets out the consequences of verifying a document containing a false statement without an honest belief in its truth.

(For information about statements of truth see Part 22 and the practice direction which supplements it.)

Information

3   Under Rule 35.9 the court may direct a party with access to information which is not reasonably available to another party to serve on that other party a document which records the information. The document served must include sufficient details of all the facts, tests, experiments and assumptions which underlie any part of the information to enable the party on whom it is served to make, or to obtain, a proper interpretation of the information and an assessment of its significance.

Instructions

4   The instructions referred to in paragraph 2.2(3) will not be protected by privilege (see rule 35.10(4)). But cross-examination of the expert on the contents of his instructions will not be allowed unless the court permits it (or unless the party who gave the instructions consents to it). Before it gives permission the court must be satisfied that there are reasonable grounds to consider that the statement in the report of the substance of the instructions is inaccurate or incomplete. If the court is so satisfied, it will allow the cross-examination where it appears to be in the interests of justice to do so.

Questions to Experts

5.1 Questions asked for the purpose of clarifying the expert's report (see rule 35.6) should be put, in writing, to the expert not later than 28 days after receipt of the expert's report (see paragraphs 1.2 to 1.5 above as to verification).

5.2 Where a party sends a written question or questions direct to an expert, a copy of the questions should, at the same time, be sent to the other party or parties.

5.3 The party or parties instructing the expert must pay any fees charged by that expert for answering questions put under rule 35.6. This does not affect any decision of the court as to the party who is ultimately to bear the expert's costs.

Single expert

6 Where the court has directed that the evidence on a particular issue is to be given by one expert only (rule 35.7) but there are a number of disciplines relevant to that issue, a leading expert in the dominant discipline should be identified as the single expert. He should prepare the general part of the report and be responsible for annexing or incorporating the contents of any reports from experts in other disciplines.

Orders

6A Where an order requires an act to be done by an expert, or otherwise affects an expert, the party instructing that expert must serve a copy of the order on the expert instructed by him. In the case of a jointly instructed expert, the claimant must serve the order.

Assessors

7.1 An assessor may be appointed to assist the court under rule 35.15. Not less than 21 days before making any such appointment, the court will notify each party in writing of the name of the proposed assessor, of the matter in respect of which the assistance of the assessor will be sought and of the qualifications of the assessor to give that assistance.

7.2 Where any person has been proposed for appointment as an assessor, objection to him, either personally or in respect of his qualification, may be taken by any party.

7.3 Any such objection must be made in writing and filed with the court within 7 days of receipt of the notification referred to in paragraph 6.1 and will be taken into account by the court in deciding whether or not to make the appointment (section 63(5) of the County Courts Act 1984).

7.4 Copies of any report prepared by the assessor will be sent to each of the parties but the assessor will not give oral evidence or be open to cross-examination or questioning.

Appendix 3
Protocol for the Instruction of Experts to give Evidence in Civil Claims

The text of the Protocol for the Instruction of Experts to give Evidence in Civil Claims is reproduced here with permission from the Civil Justice Council.

1. Introduction

Expert witnesses perform a vital role in civil litigation. It is essential that both those who instruct experts and experts themselves are given clear guidance as to what they are expected to do in civil proceedings. The purpose of this Protocol is to provide such guidance. It has been drafted by the Civil Justice Council and reflects the rules and practice directions current [in June 2005], replacing the Code of Guidance on Expert Evidence. The authors of the Protocol wish to acknowledge the valuable assistance they obtained by drawing on earlier documents produced by the Academy of Experts and the Expert Witness Institute, as well as suggestions made by the Clinical Dispute Forum. The Protocol has been approved by the Master of the Rolls.

2. Aims of Protocol

2.1 This Protocol offers guidance to experts and to those instructing them in the interpretation of and compliance with Part 35 of the Civil Procedure Rules (CPR 35) and its associated Practice Direction (PD 35) and to further the objectives of the Civil Procedure Rules in general. It is intended to assist in the interpretation of those provisions in the interests of good practice but it does not replace them. It sets out standards for the use of experts and the conduct of experts and those who instruct them. The existence of this Protocol does not remove the need for experts and those who instruct them to be familiar with CPR35 and PD35.

2.2 Experts and those who instruct them should also bear in mind para 1.4 of the Practice Direction on Protocols which contains the following objectives, namely to:

(a) encourage the exchange of early and full information about the expert issues involved in a prospective legal claim;

(b) enable the parties to avoid or reduce the scope of litigation by agreeing the whole or part of an expert issue before commencement of proceedings; and

(c) support the efficient management of proceedings where litigation cannot be avoided.

3. Application

3.1 This Protocol applies to any steps taken for the purpose of civil proceedings by experts or those who instruct them on or after 5th September 2005.

3.2 It applies to all experts who are, or who may be, governed by CPR Part 35 and to those who instruct them. Experts are governed by Part 35 if they are or have been instructed to give or prepare evidence for the purpose of civil proceedings in a court in England and Wales (CPR 35.2).

3.3 Experts, and those instructing them, should be aware that some cases may be 'specialist proceedings' (CPR 49) where there are modifications to the Civil Procedure Rules. Proceedings may also be governed by other Protocols. Further, some courts have published their own Guides which supplement the Civil Procedure Rules for proceedings in those courts. They contain provisions affecting expert evidence. Expert witnesses and those instructing them should be familiar with them when they are relevant.

3.4 Courts may take into account any failure to comply with this Protocol when making orders in relation to costs, interest, time limits, the stay of proceedings and whether to order a party to pay a sum of money into court.

Limitation

3.5 If, as a result of complying with any part of this Protocol, claims would or might be time barred under any provision in the Limitation Act 1980, or any other legislation that imposes a time limit for the bringing an action, claimants may commence proceedings without complying with this Protocol. In such circumstances, claimants who commence proceedings without complying with all, or any part, of this Protocol must apply, giving notice to all other parties, to the court for directions as to the timetable and form of procedure to be adopted, at the same time as they request the court to issue proceedings. The court may consider whether to order a stay of the whole or part of the proceedings pending compliance with this Protocol and may make orders in relation to costs.

4. Duties of experts

4.1 Experts always owe a duty to exercise reasonable skill and care to those instructing them, and to comply with any relevant professional code of ethics. However when they are instructed to give or prepare evidence for the purpose of civil proceedings in England and Wales they have an overriding duty to help the court on matters within their expertise (CPR 35.3). This duty overrides any obligation to the person instructing or paying them. Experts must not serve the exclusive interest of those who retain them.

4.2 Experts should be aware of the overriding objective that courts deal with cases justly. This includes dealing with cases proportionately, expeditiously and fairly (CPR 1.1). Experts are under an obligation to assist the court so as to enable them to deal with cases in accordance with the overriding objective. However the overriding objective does not impose on experts any duty to act as mediators between the parties or require them to trespass on the role of the court in deciding facts.

4.3 Experts should provide opinions which are independent, regardless of the pressures of litigation. In this context, a useful test of 'independence' is that the expert would express the same opinion if given the same instructions by an opposing party. Experts should not take it upon themselves to promote the point of view of the party instructing them or engage in the role of advocates.

4.4 Experts should confine their opinions to matters which are material to the disputes between the parties and provide opinions only in relation to matters which lie within their expertise. Experts should indicate without delay where particular questions or issues fall outside their expertise.

4.5 Experts should take into account all material facts before them at the time that they give their opinion. Their reports should set out those facts and any literature or any other material on which they have relied in forming their opinions. They should indicate if an opinion is provisional, or qualified, or where they consider that further information is required or if, for any other reason, they are not satisfied that an opinion can be expressed finally and without qualification.

4.6 Experts should inform those instructing them without delay of any change in their opinions on any material matter and the reason for it.

4.7 Experts should be aware that any failure by them to comply with the Civil Procedure Rules or court orders or any excessive delay for which they are responsible may result in the parties who instructed them being penalised in costs and even, in extreme cases, being debarred from placing the experts' evidence before the court. In *Phillips v Symes* Peter Smith J held that courts may also make orders for costs (under section 51 of the Supreme Court Act 1981) directly against expert witnesses who by their evidence cause significant expense to be incurred, and do so in flagrant and reckless disregard of their duties to the Court.

5. Conduct of Experts instructed only to advise

5.1 Part 35 only applies where experts are instructed to give opinions which are relied on for the purposes of court proceedings. Advice which the parties do not intend to adduce in litigation is likely to be confidential; the Protocol does not apply in these circumstances .

5.2 The same applies where, after the commencement of proceedings, experts are instructed only to advise (e.g. to comment upon a single joint expert's report) and not to give or prepare evidence for use in the proceedings.

5.3 However this Protocol does apply if experts who were formerly instructed only to advise are later instructed to give or prepare evidence for the purpose of civil proceedings.

6. The Need for Experts

6.1 Those intending to instruct experts to give or prepare evidence for the purpose of civil proceedings should consider whether expert evidence is appropriate, taking account of the principles set out in CPR Parts 1 and 35, and in particular whether:

(a) it is relevant to a matter which is in dispute between the parties.

(b) it is reasonably required to resolve the proceedings (CPR 35.1);

(c) the expert has expertise relevant to the issue on which an opinion is sought;

(d) the expert has the experience, expertise and training appropriate to the value, complexity and importance of the case; and whether

(e) these objects can be achieved by the appointment of a single joint expert (see section 17 below).

6.2 Although the court's permission is not generally required to instruct an expert, the court's permission is required before experts can be called to give evidence or their evidence can be put in (CPR 35.4).

7. The appointment of experts

7.1 Before experts are formally instructed or the court's permission to appoint named experts is sought, the following should be established:

(a) that they have the appropriate expertise and experience;

(b) that they are familiar with the general duties of an expert;

(c) that they can produce a report, deal with questions and have discussions with other experts within a reasonable time and at a cost proportionate to the matters in issue;

(d) a description of the work required;

(e) whether they are available to attend the trial, if attendance is required; and

(f) there is no potential conflict of interest.

7.2 Terms of appointment should be agreed at the outset and should normally include:

(a) the capacity in which the expert is to be appointed (e.g. party appointed expert, single joint expert or expert advisor);

(b) the services required of the expert (e.g. provision of expert's report, answering questions in writing, attendance at meetings and attendance at court);

(c) time for delivery of the report;

(d) the basis of the expert's charges (either daily or hourly rates and an estimate of the time likely to be required, or a total fee for the services);

(e) travelling expenses and disbursements;

(f) cancellation charges;

(g) any fees for attending court;

(h) time for making the payment; and

(i) whether fees are to be paid by a third party.

(j) if a party is publicly funded, whether or not the expert's charges will be subject to assessment by a costs officer.

7.3 As to the appointment of single joint experts, see section 17 below.

7.4 When necessary, arrangements should be made for dealing with questions to experts and discussions between experts, including any directions given by the court, and provision should be made for the cost of this work.

7.5 Experts should be informed regularly about deadlines for all matters concerning them. Those instructing experts should promptly send them copies of all court orders and directions which may affect the preparation of their reports or any other matters concerning their obligations.

Conditional and Contingency Fees

7.6 Payments contingent upon the nature of the expert evidence given in legal proceedings, or upon the outcome of a case, must not be offered or accepted. To do so would contravene experts' overriding duty to the court and compromise their duty of independence.

7.7 Agreement to delay payment of experts' fees until after the conclusion of cases is permissible as long as the amount of the fee does not depend on the outcome of the case.

8. Instructions

8.1 Those instructing experts should ensure that they give clear instructions, including the following:

(a) basic information, such as names, addresses, telephone numbers, dates of birth and dates of incidents;

(b) the nature and extent of the expertise which is called for;

(c) the purpose of requesting the advice or report, a description of the matter(s) to be investigated, the principal known issues and the identity of all parties;

(d) the statement(s) of case (if any), those documents which form part of standard disclosure and witness statements which are relevant to the advice or report;

(e) where proceedings have not been started, whether proceedings are being contemplated and, if so, whether the expert is asked only for advice;

(f) an outline programme, consistent with good case

management and the expert's availability, for the completion and delivery of each stage of the expert's work; and

(g) where proceedings have been started, the dates of any hearings (including any Case Management Conferences and/or Pre-Trial Reviews), the name of the court, the claim number and the track to which the claim has been allocated.

8.2 Experts who do not receive clear instructions should request clarification and may indicate that they are not prepared to act unless and until such clear instructions are received.

8.3 As to the instruction of single joint experts, see section 17 below.

9. Experts' Acceptance of Instructions

9.1 Experts should confirm without delay whether or not they accept instructions. They should also inform those instructing them (whether on initial instruction or at any later stage) without delay if:

(a) instructions are not acceptable because, for example, they require work that falls outside their expertise, impose unrealistic deadlines, or are insufficiently clear;

(b) they consider that instructions are or have become insufficient to complete the work;

(c) they become aware that they may not be able to fulfil any of the terms of appointment;

(d) the instructions and/or work have, for any reason, placed them in conflict with their duties as an expert; or

(e) they are not satisfied that they can comply with any orders that have been made.

9.2 Experts must neither express an opinion outside the scope of their field of expertise, nor accept any instructions to do so.

10. Withdrawal

10.1 Where experts' instructions remain incompatible with their duties, whether through incompleteness, a conflict between their duty to the court and their instructions, or for any other substantial and significant reason, they may consider withdrawing from the case. However, experts should not withdraw without first discussing the position fully with those who instruct them and considering carefully whether it would be more appropriate to make a written request for directions from the court. If experts do withdraw, they must give formal written notice to those instructing them.

11. Experts' Right to ask Court for Directions

11.1 Experts may request directions from the court to assist them in carrying out their functions as experts. Experts should normally discuss such matters with those who instruct them before making any such request. Unless the court otherwise orders, any proposed request for directions should be copied to the party instructing the expert at least seven days before filing any request to the court, and to all other parties at least four days before filing it. (CPR 35.14).

11.2 Requests to the court for directions should be made by letter, containing.
   (a) the title of the claim;
   (b) the claim number of the case;
   (c) the name of the expert;
   (d) full details of why directions are sought; and
   (e) copies of any relevant documentation.

12. Power of the Court to Direct a Party to Provide Information

12.1 If experts consider that those instructing them have not provided information which they require, they may, after discussion with those instructing them and giving notice, write to the court to seek directions (CPR 35.14).

12.2 Experts and those who instruct them should also be aware of CPR 35.9. This provides that where one party has access to information which is not readily available to the other party, the court may direct the party who has access to the information to prepare, file and copy to the other party a document recording the information. If experts require such information which has not been disclosed, they should discuss the position with those instructing them without delay, so that a request for the information can be made, and, if not forthcoming, an application can be made to the court. Unless a document appears to be essential, experts should assess the cost and time involved in the production of a document and whether its provision would be proportionate in the context of the case.

13. Contents of Experts' Reports

13.1 The content and extent of experts' reports should be governed by the scope of their instructions and general obligations, the contents of CPR 35 and PD35 and their overriding duty to the court.

13.2 In preparing reports, experts should maintain professional objectivity and impartiality at all times.

13.3 PD 35, para 2 provides that experts' reports should be addressed to the court and gives detailed directions about the form and content of such reports. All experts and those who instruct them should ensure that they are familiar with these requirements.

13.4 Model forms of Experts' Reports are available from bodies such as the Academy of Experts or the Expert Witness Institute.

13.5 Experts' reports must contain statements that they understand their duty to the court and have complied and will continue to comply with that duty (PD35 para 2.2(9)). They must also be verified by a statement of truth. The form of the statement of truth is as follows:

'I confirm that insofar as the facts stated in my report are within my own knowledge I have made clear which they are and I believe them to be true, and that the opinions I have expressed represent my true and complete professional opinion.'

This wording is mandatory and must not be modified.

Qualifications

13.6 The details of experts' qualifications to be given in reports should be commensurate with the nature and complexity of the case. It may be sufficient merely to state academic and professional qualifications. However, where highly specialised expertise is called for, experts should include the detail of particular training and/or experience that qualifies them to provide that highly specialised evidence.

Tests

13.7 Where tests of a scientific or technical nature have been carried out, experts should state:
(a) the methodology used; and
(b) by whom the tests were undertaken and under whose supervision, summarising their respective qualifications and experience.

Reliance on the work of others

13.8 Where experts rely in their reports on literature or other material and cite the opinions of others without having verified them, they must give details of those opinions relied on. It is likely to assist the court if the qualifications of the originator(s) are also stated.

Facts

13.9 When addressing questions of fact and opinion, experts should keep the two separate and discrete.

13.10 Experts must state those facts (whether assumed or otherwise) upon which their opinions are based. They must distinguish clearly between those facts which experts know to be true and those facts which they assume.

13.11 Where there are material facts in dispute experts should express separate opinions on each hypothesis put forward. They should not express a view in favour of one or other disputed version of the facts unless, as a result of particular expertise and experience, they consider one set of facts as being improbable or less probable, in which case they may express that view, and should give reasons for holding it.

Range of opinion

13.12 If the mandatory summary of the range of opinion is based on published sources, experts should explain those sources and, where appropriate, state the qualifications of the originator(s) of the opinions from which they differ, particularly if such opinions represent a well-established school of thought.

13.13 Where there is no available source for the range of opinion, experts may need to express opinions on what they believe to be the range which other experts would arrive at if asked. In those circumstances, experts should make it clear that the range that they summarise is based on their own judgement and explain the basis of that judgement.

Conclusions

13.14 A summary of conclusions is mandatory. The summary should be at the end of the report after all the reasoning. There may be cases, however, where the benefit to the court is heightened by placing a short summary at the beginning of the report whilst giving the full conclusions at the end. For example, it can assist with the comprehension of the analysis and with the absorption of the detailed facts if the court is told at the outset of the direction in which the report's logic will flow in cases involving highly complex matters which fall outside the general knowledge of the court.

Basis of report: material instructions

13.15 The mandatory statement of the substance of all material instructions should not be incomplete or otherwise tend to mislead. The imperative is transparency. The term 'instructions' includes all material which solicitors place in front of experts in order to gain advice. The omission from the statement of 'off-the-record' oral instructions is not permitted. Courts may allow cross-examination about the instructions if there are reasonable grounds to consider that the statement may be inaccurate or incomplete.

14. After receipt of experts' reports

14.1 Following the receipt of experts' reports, those instructing them should advise the experts as soon as reasonably practicable whether, and if so when, the report will be disclosed to other parties; and, if so disclosed, the date of actual disclosure.

14.2 If experts' reports are to be relied upon, and if experts are to give oral evidence, those instructing them should give the experts the opportunity to consider and comment upon other reports within their area of expertise and which deal with relevant issues at the earliest opportunity.

14.3 Those instructing experts should keep experts informed of the progress of cases, including amendments to statements of case relevant to experts' opinion.

14.4 If those instructing experts become aware of material changes in circumstances or that relevant information within their control was not previously provided to experts, they should without delay instruct experts to review, and if necessary, update the contents of their reports.

15. Amendment of reports

15.1 It may become necessary for experts to amend their reports:

(a) as a result of an exchange of questions and answers;

(b) following agreements reached at meetings between experts; or

(c) where further evidence or documentation is disclosed.

15.2 Experts should not be asked to, and should not, amend, expand or alter any parts of reports in a manner which distorts their true opinion, but may be invited to amend or expand reports to ensure accuracy, internal consistency, completeness and relevance to the issues and clarity. Although experts should generally follow the recommendations of solicitors with regard to the form of reports, they should form their own independent views as to the opinions and contents expressed in their reports and exclude any suggestions which do not accord with their views.

15.3 Where experts change their opinion following a meeting of experts, a simple signed and dated addendum or memorandum to that effect is generally sufficient. In some cases, however, the benefit to the court of having an amended report may justify the cost of making the amendment.

15.4 Where experts significantly alter their opinion, as a result of new evidence or because evidence on which they relied has become unreliable, or for any other reason, they should amend their reports to reflect that fact. Amended reports should include reasons for amendments. In such circumstances those instructing experts should inform other parties as soon as possible of any change of opinion.

15.5 When experts intend to amend their reports, they should inform those instructing them without delay and give reasons. They should provide the amended version (or an addendum or memorandum) clearly marked as such as quickly as possible.

16. Written Questions to Experts

16.1   The procedure for putting written questions to experts (CPR 35.6) is intended to facilitate the clarification of opinions and issues after experts' reports have been served. Experts have a duty to provide answers to questions properly put. Where they fail to do so, the court may impose sanctions against the party instructing the expert, and, if, there is continued non-compliance, debar a party from relying on the report. Experts should copy their answers to those instructing them.

16.2   Experts' answers to questions automatically become part of their reports. They are covered by the statement of truth and form part of the expert evidence.

16.3   Where experts believe that questions put are not properly directed to the clarification of the report, or are disproportionate, or have been asked out of time, they should discuss the questions with those instructing them and, if appropriate, those asking the questions. Attempts should be made to resolve such problems without the need for an application to the court for directions.

Written requests for directions in relation to questions

16.4   If those instructing experts do not apply to the court in respect of questions, but experts still believe that questions are improper or out of time, experts may file written requests with the court for directions to assist in carrying out their functions as experts (CPR 35.14). See Section 11 above.

17. Single Joint Experts

17.1   CPR 35 and PD35 deal extensively with the instruction and use of joint experts by the parties and the powers of the court to order their use (see CPR 35.7 and 35.8, PD35, para 5).

17.2   The Civil Procedure Rules encourage the use of joint experts. Wherever possible a joint report should be obtained. Consideration should therefore be given by all parties to the appointment of single joint experts in all cases where a court might direct such an appointment. Single joint experts are the norm in cases allocated to the small claims track and the fast track.

17.3   Where, in the early stages of a dispute, examinations, investigations, tests, site inspections, experiments, preparation of photographs, plans or other similar preliminary expert tasks are necessary, consideration should be given to the instruction of a single joint expert, especially where such matters are not, at that stage, expected to be contentious as between the parties. The objective of such an appointment should be to agree or to narrow issues.

17.5   Experts who have previously advised a party (whether in the same case or otherwise) should only be proposed as single joint experts if other parties are given all relevant information about the previous involvement.

17.6   The appointment of a single joint expert does not prevent parties from instructing their own experts to advise (but the costs of such expert advisers may not be recoverable in the case).

Joint instructions

17.7   The parties should try to agree joint instructions to single joint experts, but, in default of agreement, each party may give instructions. In particular, all parties should try to agree what documents should be included with instructions and what assumptions single joint experts should make.

17.8   Where the parties fail to agree joint instructions, they should try to agree where the areas of disagreement lie and their instructions should make this clear. If separate instructions are given, they should be copied at the same time to the other instructing parties.

17.9   Where experts are instructed by two or more parties, the terms of appointment should, unless the court has directed otherwise, or the parties have agreed otherwise, include:

(a) a statement that all the instructing parties are jointly and severally liable to pay the experts' fees and, accordingly, that experts' invoices should be sent simultaneously to all instructing parties or their solicitors (as appropriate); and

(b) a statement as to whether any order has been made limiting the amount of experts' fees and expenses (CPR 35.8(4)(a)).

17.10 Where instructions have not been received by the expert from one or more of the instructing parties the expert should give notice (normally at least 7 days) of a deadline to all instructing parties for the receipt by the expert of such instructions. Unless the instructions are received within the deadline the expert may begin work. In the event that instructions are received after the deadline but before the signing off of the report the expert should consider whether it is practicable to comply with those instructions without adversely affecting the timetable set for delivery of the report and in such a manner as to comply with the proportionality principle. An expert who decides to issue a report without taking into account instructions received after the deadline should inform the parties who may apply to the court for directions. In either event the report must show clearly that the expert did not receive instructions within the deadline, or, as the case may be, at all.

Conduct of the single joint expert

17.11 Single joint experts should keep all instructing parties informed of any material steps that they may be taking by, for example, copying all correspondence to those instructing them.

17.12 Single joint experts are Part 35 experts and so have an overriding duty to the court. They are the parties' appointed experts and therefore owe an equal duty to all parties. They should maintain independence, impartiality and transparency at all times.

17.13 Single joint experts should not attend any meeting or conference which is not a joint one, unless all the parties have agreed in writing or the court has directed that such a meeting may be held and who is to pay the experts' fees for the meeting.

17.14 Single joint experts may request directions from the court – see Section 11 above.

17.15 Single joint experts should serve their reports simultaneously on all instructing parties. They should provide a single report even though they may have received instructions which contain areas of conflicting fact or allegation. If conflicting instructions lead to different opinions (for example, because the instructions require experts to make different assumptions of fact), reports may need to contain more than one set of opinions on any issue. It is for the court to determine the facts.

Cross-examination

17.16 Single joint experts do not normally give oral evidence at trial but if they do, all parties may cross-examine them. In general written questions (CPR 35.6) should be put to single joint experts before requests are made for them to attend court for the purpose of cross-examination.

18. Discussions between Experts

18.1 The court has powers to direct discussions between experts for the purposes set out in the Rules (CPR 35.12). Parties may also agree that discussions take place between their experts.

18.2 Where single joint experts have been instructed but parties have, with the permission of the court, instructed their own additional Part 35 experts, there may, if the court so orders or the parties agree, be discussions between the single joint experts and the additional Part 35 experts. Such discussions should be confined to those matters within the remit of the additional Part 35 experts or as ordered by the court.

18.3   The purpose of discussions between experts should be, wherever possible, to:
(a) identify and discuss the expert issues in the proceedings;
(b) reach agreed opinions on those issues, and, if that is not possible, to narrow the issues in the case;
(c) identify those issues on which they agree and disagree and summarise their reasons for disagreement on any issue; and
(d) identify what action, if any, may be taken to resolve any of the outstanding issues between the parties.

Arrangements for discussions between experts

18.4   Arrangements for discussions between experts should be proportionate to the value of cases. In small claims and fast-track cases there should not normally be meetings between experts. Where discussion is justified in such cases, telephone discussion or an exchange of letters should, in the interests of proportionality, usually suffice. In multi-track cases, discussion may be face to face, but the practicalities or the proportionality principle may require discussions to be by telephone or video conference.

18.5   The parties, their lawyers and experts should co-operate to produce the agenda for any discussion between experts, although primary responsibility for preparation of the agenda should normally lie with the parties' solicitors.

18.6   The agenda should indicate what matters have been agreed and summarise concisely those which are in issue. It is often helpful for it to include questions to be answered by the experts. If agreement cannot be reached promptly or a party is unrepresented, the court may give directions for the drawing up of the agenda. The agenda should be circulated to experts and those instructing them to allow sufficient time for the experts to prepare for the discussion.

18.7   Those instructing experts must not instruct experts to avoid reaching agreement (or to defer doing so) on any matter within the experts' competence. Experts are not permitted to accept such instructions.

18.8   The parties' lawyers may only be present at discussions between experts if all the parties agree or the court so orders. If lawyers do attend, they should not normally intervene except to answer questions put to them by the experts or to advise about the law.

18.9   The content of discussions between experts should not be referred to at trial unless the parties agree (CPR 35.12(4)). It is good practice for any such agreement to be in writing.

18.10   At the conclusion of any discussion between experts, a statement should be prepared setting out:

(a)   a list of issues that have been agreed, including, in each instance, the basis of agreement;

(b)   a list of issues that have not been agreed, including, in each instance, the basis of disagreement;

(c)   a list of any further issues that have arisen that were not included in the original agenda for discussion;

(d)   a record of further action, if any, to be taken or recommended, including as appropriate the holding of further discussions between experts.

18.11   The statement should be agreed and signed by all the parties to the discussion as soon as may be practicable.

18.12   Agreements between experts during discussions do not bind the parties unless the parties expressly agree to be bound by the agreement (CPR 35.12(5)). However, in view of the overriding objective, parties should give careful consideration before refusing to be bound by such an agreement and be able to explain their refusal should it become relevant to the issue of costs.

19. Attendance of Experts at Court

19.1   Experts instructed in cases have an obligation to attend court if called upon to do so and accordingly should ensure that those instructing them are always aware of their dates to be avoided and take all reasonable steps to be available.

19.2 Those instructing experts should:
   (a) ascertain the availability of experts before trial dates are fixed;
   (b) keep experts updated with timetables (including the dates and times experts are to attend) and the location of the court;
   (c) give consideration, where appropriate, to experts giving evidence via a video-link.
   (d) inform experts immediately if trial dates are vacated.

19.3 Experts should normally attend court without the need for the service of witness summonses, but on occasion they may be served to require attendance (CPR 34). The use of witness summonses does not affect the contractual or other obligations of the parties to pay experts' fees.

Index

The Case in Point series

The *Case in Point* series is an exiting new set of concise practical
guides to legal issues in land, property and construction. Written
for the property professional, they get straight to the key issues in
a refreshingly jargon-free style.

Areas covered:

Negligence in Valuation and Surveys
Stock code: 6388
Published: December 2002

Party Walls
Stock code: 7269
Published: May 2004

Service Charges
Stock code: 7272
Published: June 2004

Estate Agency
Stock code: 7472
Published: July 2004

Rent Review
Stock code: 8531
Published: May 2005

Publishing soon:
Lease Renewal
VAT in Property and Construction

If you would like to be kept informed when new *Case in Point* titles
are published, please e-mail **rbmarketing@rics.org.uk**

How to order:
All RICS Books titles can be ordered direct by:
☎   Telephoning 0870 333 1600 (Option 3)
🖱   Online at www.ricsbooks.com
📠   E-mail mailorder@rics.org.uk